GRAMMAR
MADE EASY
Beginner

by Mat Wilton

Publisher information and year

ISBN-13: 978-0-6453950-0-6

Copyright © Mat Wilton 2022

The right of Mat Wilton to be identified as the author of this work has been asserted by him in accordance with the Copyright, Designs and Patents Act 1988

All rights reserved. No part of this publication may be reproduced, stored in a retrieval system, or transmitted, in any form, or by any means (electronic, mechanical, photocopying, recording or otherwise) without the prior written permission of the publisher.

Designations used by companies to distinguish their products are often claimed as trademarks. All brand names and product names used in this book are trade names, service marks, trademarks or registered trademarks of their respective owners. The publisher is not associated with any product or vendor mentioned in this book. This publication is designed to provide accurate and authoritative information in regard to the subject matter covered. It is sold on the understanding that the publisher is not engaged in rendering professional services. If professional advice or other expert assistance is required, the services of a competent professional should be sought.

This book is sold subject to the condition that it shall not, by way of trade or otherwise, be lent, hired out, or otherwise circulated without the publisher's prior consent in any form of binding or cover other than that in which it is published and without a similar condition including this condition being imposed on the subsequent purchaser.

Contents

NOUNS

THE ADJECTIVE

THE PREPOSITION

THE VERB

THE CONJUNCTION

07 HOW PICTURES WORK
The all you need to know guide on how to use pictures.

09 PICTURE 1: Nouns

13 PICTURE 2: The Spotlight

17 PICTURE 3: The Shadow On The Noun

21 PICTURE 4: The Determiner

27 PICTURE 5: The Adjective

31 PICTURE 6: The Preposition

37 PICTURE 7: The Verb

41 PICTURE 8a: The Adverb with Adjectives

45 PICTURE 8b: The Adverb with Verbs

49 PICTURE 9: The Conjunction

55 PICTURE 10: The Relative Pronoun And Its Clause

59 ADDITIONAL EXERCISES

THE RELATIVE PRONOUN

"Today Grammar is barely living and I intend to bring it to a new dawning. If you can't find the book you want to read: you've got to write it. With over 50 years of experience in teaching, I have become a grammar master by developing a new pedagogy. It has taken four years of research and development and another eight years of successful trialling to develop the Pictorial Grammar Theory."

by Mat Wilton

How PICTURES work

What motivated me to write a book about grammar? I was editing university papers for students who were passing well. Their grammar was shocking, yet I could pull their texts around, making the language quite palatable to a tertiary marker. I must know something worth imparting. How did we get to a state where we have forgotten the importance of grammar?!!!

Grammar is finite: there are no new discoveries being made in grammar. Therefore, I reasoned, once I had the pathway into its labyrinth, there would be a way through. The challenge was to make the path... easy. There are a lot of very hard books out there on grammar, especially with the title of "easy". My book had to be something different, good, and it had to be effective.

The book became a steady investment of my time. For the next four years, I rediscovered the language that I'd learnt at my mother's knee, as I researched the structure of the English language. I was writing a book about grammar that I understood, with a surety that I could teach to my students.

But it was, despite my passion, just another book about grammar. However, I'd finished decorating a page with a magnifying glass over structure class words, with little stick figures running all around, sitting on letters, sliding down slopes when the, you know, the switch was thrown and the prototype was born. Pictorial Grammar Theory.

Someone has said that learning is about changing one's way of experiencing the phenomenon. I didn't want to write text: *I wanted to write on text*. There are only a small number of functions happening in a sentence: the roles for words are limited. I embarked to represent these words as a visual concept: I wanted an image that, every time it was drawn, reinforced the concept of the word: the picture actually meant something!

There is a close relationship between movement and cognition, the best learning is active and the order of learning is beneficial. The constructivists, (Montessori, Brunner, Dewey, Piaget) espouse that children can create knowledge. People learn best when they are actively engaged. Deep concentration is essential and comes about through working with their hands on the materials (on the text).

In this book there are manageable steps in each area aimed at mastering the task. The motions such as "boxing the noun, growing the shadow" are carried out in a strategic sequence. The action that occurs must be connected to the mental activity going on. Children show an intense interest in language and theorists agree that gesture facilitates thought. The child needs activity focused on a task that requires movement of the hands guided by the intellect. One of the pleasures of learning is constantly having new insights into, and new ways of thinking about, things we thought we fully understood.

A sentence has a hive mentality. Don't underline a noun, circle a verb because it's pointless: it's just pulling the gang apart. A sentence walks down the road as a unified, harmonious force: every word has a role to play. There are no dents or weak spots in a sentence: it's a cunning group of words deliberately chosen to convey a meaning: and has a tight hive-minded structure, with no non-contributing parts. The knowledge of word patterns is phenomenally important.

Pictorial Grammar Theory:
Simple stories are coupled with semiotic* imagery that underlies a brand-new, innovative, and divergent pedagogy on the teaching and learning of grammar. Scarcely a word is written, as students overlay powerfully understood symbols/images upon the text: any text. The image is a synthesis of the word's function within a sentence. Sentences are transformed into a pleasing aesthetic of connected images.

*Semiotics: based on "semiosis," the relationship between a sign, an object, and a meaning.

YOU CAN FIND MORE EXERCISES AND RESOURCES AT

www.profstripes.com

GRAMMAR Made Easy

PICTURE 1: Nouns

> A noun is a word that is used to identify a person, place, emotion or object.

Nouns are our first words. If you can take a photo of something, then it is a noun: even concepts and emotions. Co-operation and happiness are nouns. Without difficulty, you can imagine photos that could be called these things.

Nouns   are the name of   things
Things   can have their   photo taken
Photos   have a   box around them

Recognising a noun is the beginning for understanding a sentence.

PAGE 9

emotions

animals

food

Noun Strategy:

There is an essential way for drawing the box:

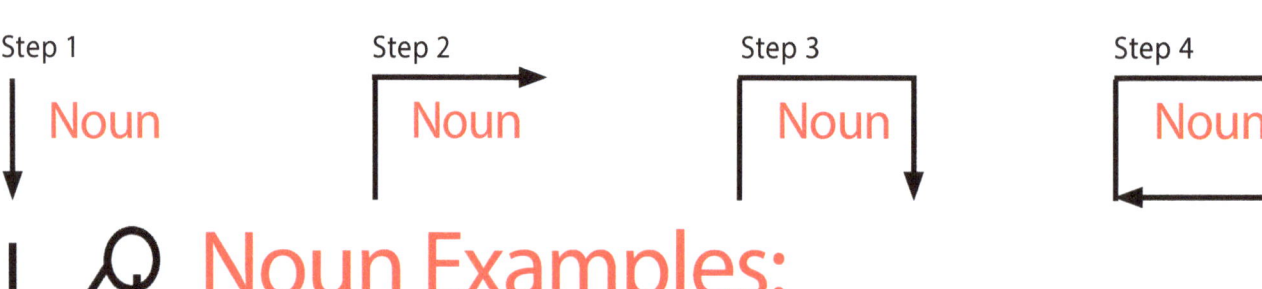

Noun Examples:

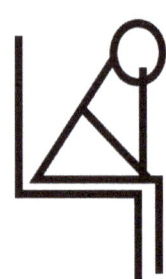

Boxing the nouns.

The poor [farmer] had a fat [cow]. The old [farmer] was a [saint].

The [cow] was a [devil] with [horns].

In the shabby [barn] by the [piles] of yellow [straw] the [cow] had a [stall].

The loose [strands] of dry [straw] made a wonderfully smart [pattern] on the [ground].

Noun Exercise

If you can take a photo of something, then that something is a noun, and the photo will have a box around it. Draw, in the correct way, a box around any words that could be nouns in the "Words" exercise and then do it for the nouns in the sentences of the stories.

Words:

highway	elephant	already	of
river	stone	very	laptop
curtain	certainly	bridge	happiness
almost	concentration	disappointment	

Story 1:

The family was going on a picnic. The car was packed with food, blankets, chairs, bats and balls. Their destination was eighteen kilometres away called, Outback Park.

Story 2:

The little pigs had backpacks, old suitcases, shabby boxes and bundles of clothes on sticks. The sad pigs had salty tears in their bloodshot eyes. Their tired mother had a loose strand of hair and a sad look on her face. On the greasy stove the saucepans were a mess.

Noun Exercise Answers

If you can take a photo of something, then that something is a noun, and the photo will have a box around it. Draw, in the correct way, a box around any words that could be nouns in the "Words" exercise and then do it for the nouns in the sentences of the stories.

Words:

highway   elephant   already   of

river   stone   very   laptop

curtain   certainly   bridge   happiness

almost   concentration   disappointment

Story 1:

The family was going on a picnic. The car was packed with food, blankets, chairs, bats and balls. Their destination was eighteen kilometres away, called Outback Park.

Story 2:

The little pigs had backpacks, old suitcases, shabby boxes and bundles of clothes on sticks. The sad pigs had salty tears in their bloodshot eyes. Their tired mother had a loose strand of hair and a sad look on her face. On the greasy stove the saucepans were a mess.

PICTURE 2: The Spotlight

> **"** On stage, the spotlight is projected onto the main character. The same can be said for a noun in a sentence. **"**

A**ny noun** can be the **main character** of a sentence. The main character gets the spotlight. A sentence can have several nouns, but only one noun will be the main character and have the spotlight.

Note: A sentence can have two spotlights, but only when it is two clauses joined by a conjunction (see Picture 9, Page 49)

farmer

leaf

food

The Spotlight Strategy:

There is an essential way for drawing the spotlight:

Step 1 — Noun
Step 2 — Noun
Step 3 — Noun
Step 4 — Noun

The Spotlight Examples:

Boxing the nouns and selecting the main character

The poor farmer had a fat cow. The old farmer was a saint.

The cow was a devil with horns.

In the shabby barn by the piles of yellow straw the cow had a stall.

The loose strands of dry straw made a wonderfully smart

pattern on the ground.

GRAMMAR Made Easy

Spotlight Exercise

Box the nouns. Add the spotlight, because any noun could be the main character. Within the sentences, there will only be one main character.

Words:

towards   about   supermarket   homework

oval   so   balloons   quite
anger   dishwasher   fondness   conclusion

softly

Story 1:

The team was going on a picnic. The bus was filled with food, drinks, nets, bats and sunscreen. The coach was driving. Reading the map was the manager.

Story 2:

The little |pigs| had |backpacks,| old |suitcases,| shabby |boxes| and |bundles| of |clothes| on |sticks.| The sad |pigs| had salty |tears| in their bloodshot |eyes.| Their tired |mother| had a loose |strand| of |hair| and a sad |look| on her |face.| On the greasy |stove| the |saucepans| were a |mess.|

Spotlight Exercise Answers

Box the nouns. Add the spotlight, because any noun could be the main character. Within the sentences, there will only be one main character.

Words:

towards   about   [supermarket]★   [homework]★

[oval]★   so   [balloons]★   quite

anger   [dishwasher]★   [fondness]★   [conclusion]★

softly

Story 1:

The [team]★ was going on a [picnic]. The [bus] was filled with [food], [drinks], [nets], [bats] and [sunscreen]. The [coach]★ was driving. Reading the [map] was the [manager]★.

Story 2:

The little [pigs]★ had [backpacks], old [suitcases], shabby [boxes] and [bundles] of [clothes] on [sticks]. The sad [pigs]★ had salty [tears] in their bloodshot [eyes]. Their tired [mother]★ had a loose [strand] of [hair] and a sad [look] on her [face]. On the greasy [stove] the [saucepans]★ were a [mess].

PICTURE 3: The Shadow On The Noun

> "All nouns cast a shadow."

The possibility of having a spotlight gives all nouns a shadow.

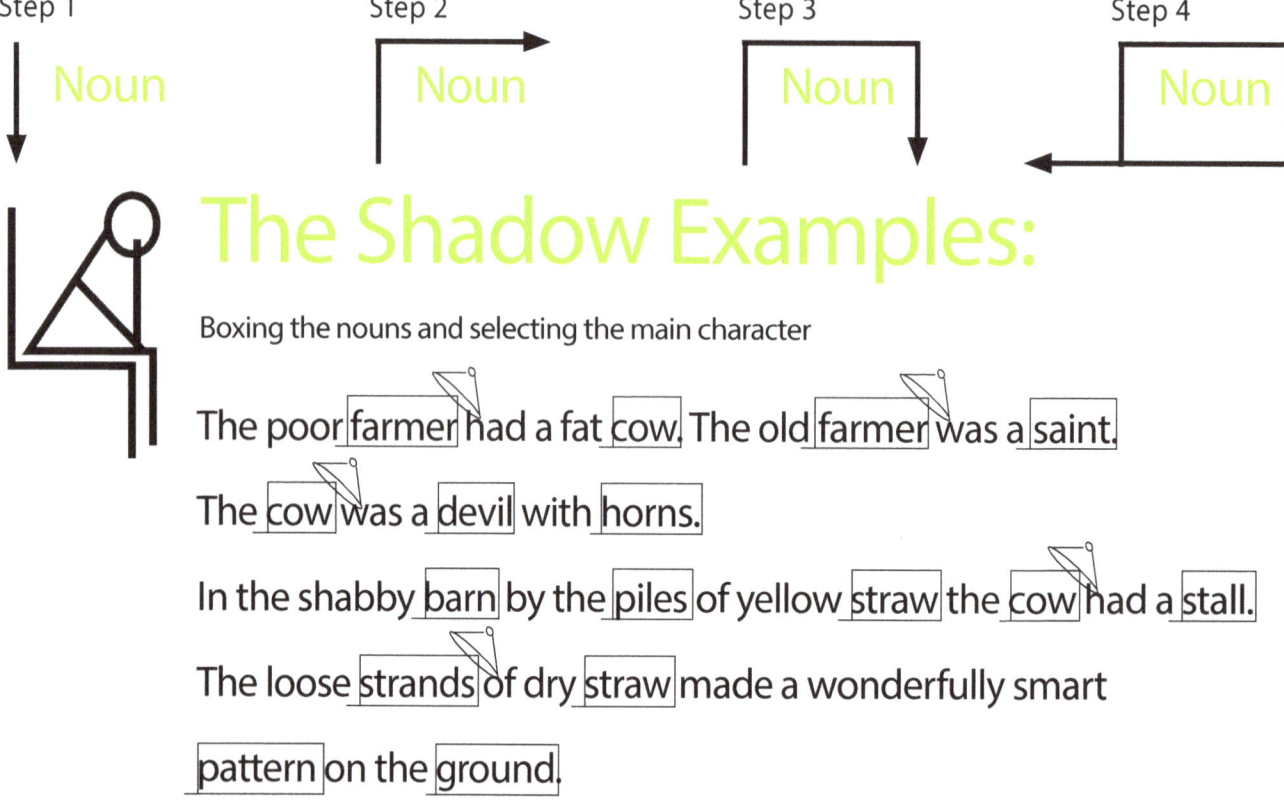

The tree (noun) casts a shadow

The Shadow On The Noun Strategy:

There is an essential way for drawing the shadow. Draw the box like before and finish off with a shadow.

Step 1   Step 2   Step 3   Step 4

Noun   Noun   Noun   Noun

The Shadow Examples:

Boxing the nouns and selecting the main character

The poor farmer had a fat cow. The old farmer was a saint.

The cow was a devil with horns.

In the shabby barn by the piles of yellow straw the cow had a stall.

The loose strands of dry straw made a wonderfully smart pattern on the ground.

The Shadow Exercise

Box the nouns and finish off with a shadow. Within the sentences, also add the spotlight to the main character.

Words:

uniform	collar	landscape	does
silly	mongoose	silliness	defence
alien	affectionately	affection	conclusion
goes	not		

Story 1:

At the beach Mum was using sunscreen on the children. The beach was covered with shells, seaweed, surfboards and noisy families. Under the umbrella Grandpa was quietly snoozing.

Story 2:

Their frail mother had a soiled apron and had a sad look on her face. On the wobbly table the empty pizza-boxes were a jumble. On the grubby benchtops the dirty plates were a mess. Under the rusty sink a skinny mouse had a crumb of stale bread in its paws. The sloppy kitchen was a disaster.

The Shadow Exercise Answers

Box the nouns and finish off with a shadow. Within the sentences, also add the spotlight to the main character.

Words:

uniform   collar   landscape   does

silly   mongoose   silliness   defence

alien   affectionately   affection   conclusion

goes   not

Story 1:

At the beach Mum was using sunscreen on the children. The beach was covered with shells, seaweed, surfboards and noisy families. Under the umbrella Grandpa was quietly snoozing.

Story 2:

Their frail mother had a soiled apron and had a sad look on her face. On the wobbly table the empty pizza-boxes were a jumble. On the grubby benchtops the dirty plates were a mess. Under the rusty sink a skinny mouse had a crumb of stale bread in its paws. The sloppy kitchen was a disaster.

PICTURE 4: The Determiner

> Not every noun needs to have a determiner. The important thing is, if the word is adding detail about the noun, then it must be riding on the noun's shadow.
>
> Adjectives ride on the noun's shadow (Picture 5).

Determiners pinpoint the noun, fine-tuning the information in the sentence. The noun's shadow grows until it stops under a determiner.

The Determiner in Use

These words often function as determiners:

a
an
the
my
this
that
those
their
our
your
his
her

Nouns Becoming Determiners

Apostrophes: this marker **'** or this marker **'** are used with the letter **S** to show ownership.

S is also used at the end of a noun to show that there is more than one.

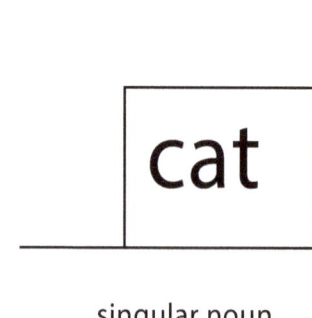

singular noun

plural noun

GRAMMAR Made Easy

Looking behind the apostrophe, will tell you the number of owners

One cat is owning one bowl, and that
singular noun has become a determiner

Many cats are owning one bowl, and the
plural noun has become a determiner

Lots of cats are owning lots of bowls

PAGE 23

The Determiner Examples:

Boxing the nouns. Notice the "owner" becoming determiners on line 5.

The poor farmer had a fat cow. This old farmer was a saint.

His cow was a devil with horns. The farmer's wife was in

the shabby barn by the piles of yellow straw the cow had a stall.

Many strands of dry straw made several intricate patterns

on the ground. The owner's animal was unnoticing of

this special effect.

The Determiner Exercise

Box the nouns and grow the shadow to finish under the determiner. Within Story 2, also add the spotlight to the main character.

Words:

another wonderful day

this monkey

the school's honest student

the most amazing opportunity

Fiona's best wishes

our special place

an exhausting holiday

my mum

Story 1:

The Zoo's entrance was crowded with an excited collection of many amazing people. Dressed as their favourite animal, these imaginative folk received some crazy discounts.

Story 2:

Their frail mother had a soiled apron and had a sad look on her face. On the wobbly table the empty pizza-boxes were a crazy jumble. On the grubby benchtops those dirty plates were a mess. Under the rusty sink a skinny mouse had a crumb of stale bread in its paws. The sloppy kitchen was a disaster.

The Determiner Exercise Answers

Box the nouns and grow the shadow to finish under the determiner. Within Story 2, also add the spotlight to the main characters.

Words:

another wonderful day

this monkeys

the school's honest student

the most amazing opportunity

Fiona's best wishes

our special place

an exhausting holiday

my mum

Story 1:

The Zoo's entrance was crowded with an excited collection of many amazing people. Dressed as their favourite animal, these imaginative folk received some crazy discounts.

Story 2:

Their frail mother had a soiled apron and had a sad look on her face. On the wobbly table the empty pizza-boxes were a crazy jumble. On the grubby benchtops those dirty plates were a mess. Under the rusty sink a skinny mouse had a crumb of stale bread in its paws. The sloppy kitchen was a disaster.

PICTURE 5: The Adjective

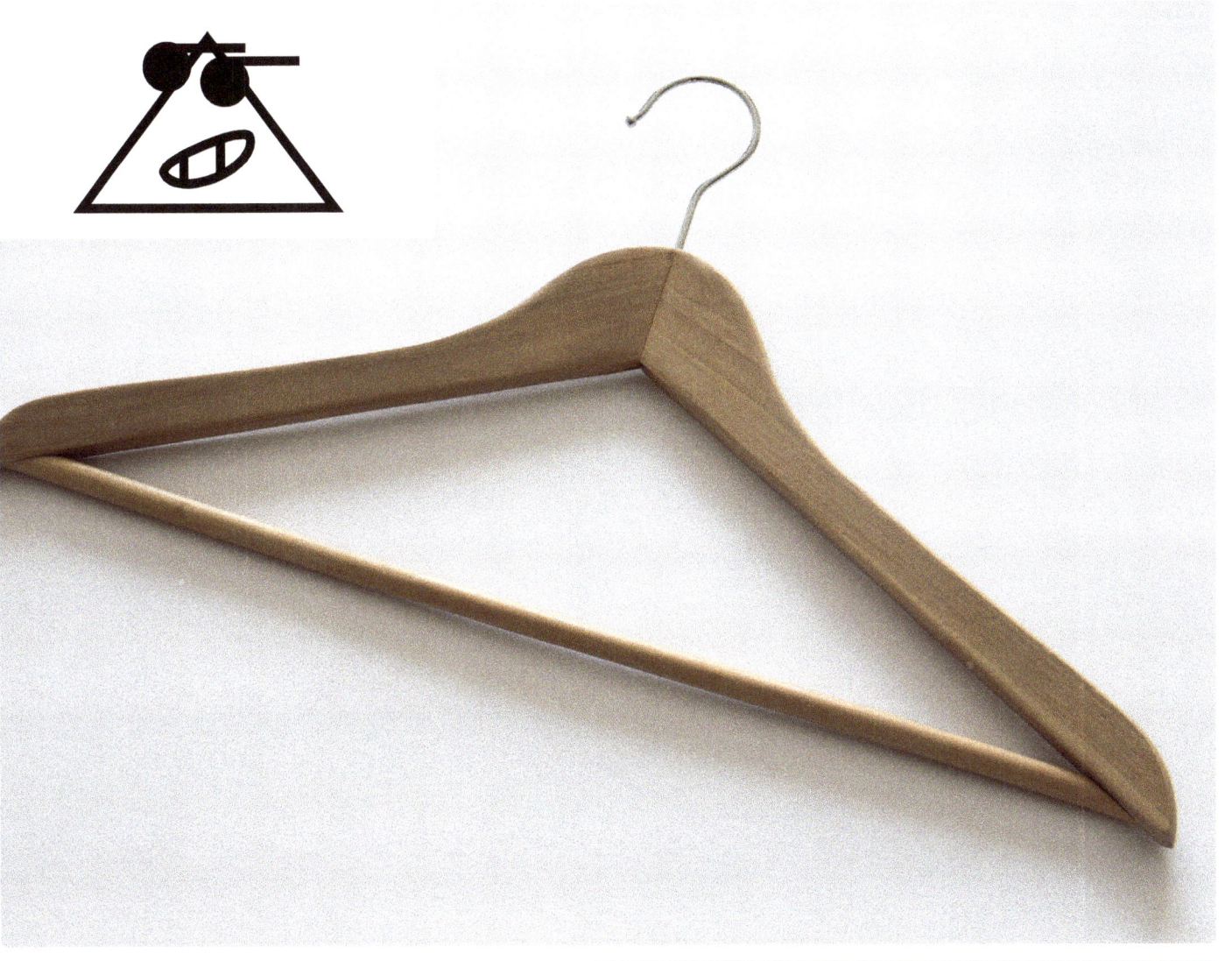

> "Adjectives advertise the noun and add the detail."

Adjectives are agents for their nouns, and ride with them on their shadow. Adjectives are important hangers on: they're coat hangers!

Adjectives sometimes complete the sentence that is started by the noun. It is still hanging out with the noun, but at the end of the sentence.

All of the pictures so far demonstrate the complete noun phrase. Noun and Noun Phrases are treated as interchangeable terms.

For simplicity the drawing can be just a triangle without the sunglasses and smile.

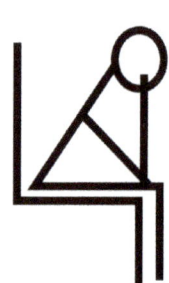

The Adjective Examples:

Boxing the nouns and adding a triangle where the adjective occurs within the sentence.

The poor farmer had a fat cow. This old farmer was a saint.

His cow was a devil with horns. The farmer's wife was nice.

In the shabby barn by the piles of yellow straw the cow had a stall.

Many strands of dry straw made several interesting patterns

on the ground. The owner's animal was unaware of

this special effect.

The Adjective Exercise

Box the nouns and grow the shadow to finish under the determiner. Within the sentences, also add the spotlight to the main character and draw a triangle to represent the adjective.

Words:

those magnificent men

Mother's magical day

your kind thoughts

Einstein's amazing imagination

many hectic moments

that golden sunset

another tiny tiny crack

Story 1:

Our Circus's biggest attraction was the dangerous trapeze. On several frightening occasions that dashing Yusef had fallen to the safety of some stretched netting under those wires.

Story 2:

Their frail mother had a soiled apron and had a sad look on her face. On the wobbly table the empty pizza-boxes were a crazy jumble. On the grubby benchtops those dirty plates were a mess. Under the rusty sink a skinny mouse had a crumb of stale bread in its paws. The sloppy kitchen was a disaster.

The Adjective Exercise Answers

Box the nouns and grow the shadow to finish under the determiner. Within the sentences, also add the spotlight to the main character and draw a triangle to represent the adjective.

Words:

those magnificent men

Mother's magical day

your kind thoughts

Einstein's amazing imagination

many hectic moments

that golden sunset

another tiny tiny crack

Story 1:

Our Circus's biggest attraction was the dangerous trapeze. On several frightening occasions that dashing Yusef had fallen to the safety of some stretched netting under those wires.

Story 2:

Their frail mother had a soiled apron and had a sad look on her face. On the wobbly table the empty pizza-boxes were a crazy jumble. On the grubby benchtops those dirty plates were a mess. Under the rusty sink a skinny mouse had a crumb of stale bread in its paws. The sloppy kitchen was a disaster.

GRAMMAR Made Easy

PICTURE 6: The Preposition

Prepositions are pictured as scissors because prepositional phrases can always be cut out of a sentence, and the sentence will still make sense.

A prepositional phrase presents a previous noun or event in more precise detail.

> "Prepositions describe the where or when of a previous noun or event."

The Preposition in Use

Prepositions, like compass points, map out:

the where-abouts (its position) of a noun, using another noun.

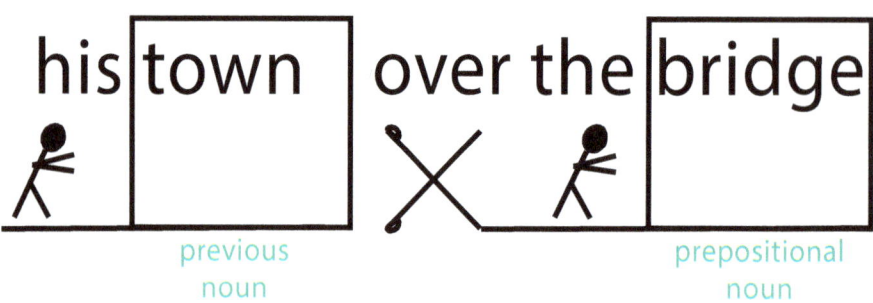

or the when-abouts (the time something happened) of an event.

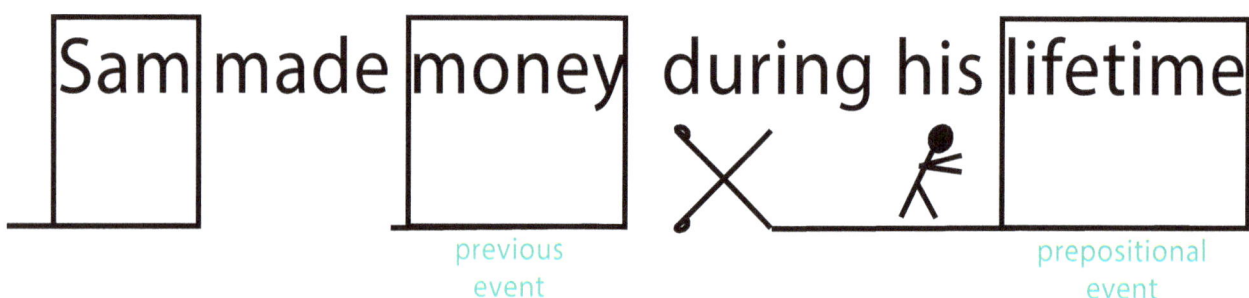

Prepositions do not function on their own. They always begin a prepositional phrase, made up of the preposition and a noun phrase.

Prepositions always have objects.

They are always:

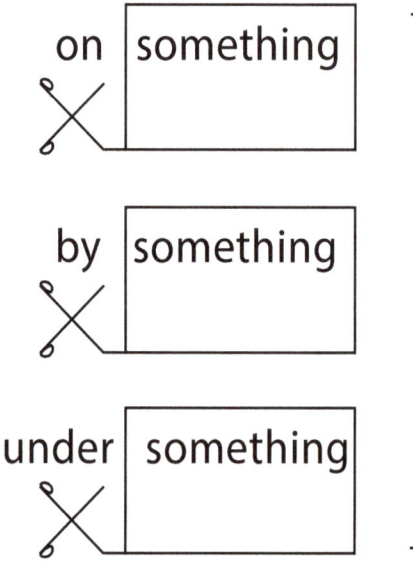

The something is always a noun. Nouns are always the object of a preposition

These words often function as prepositions:

about	despite	past
above	down	since
across	during	through
after	except	throughout
against	for	till
along	from	to
among	in	toward
around	inside	under
at	into	underneath
before	like	until
behind	near	up
beneath	of	upon
beside	off	with
between	on	within
beyond	onto	without
by	out	
	outside	
	over	

The Preposition Examples:

The examples demonstrate how prepositional phrases can bring more detail to a sentence. Adjectives still ride on the noun's shadow.

Example 1.

The poor farmer had a fat cow.

The poor farmer had a fat cow in a shabby barn.

Example 2.

This old farmer was a saint.

This old farmer was a saint with dried mud on his battered boots.

Example 3.

His cow was a devil.

His cow was a devil with horns.

✕ Knowing that you can remove the prepositional phrases, gives a rewarding 'hands-on' feeling: that you are really manipulating the sentence; enjoying a sense of being-in-control of the language.

The Preposition Exercise

Your first strategy is to box the nouns. Secondly, identify the prepositional phrases. Thirdly, cross them out. Last of all, within the stories, add the spotlight to the main character.

Words:

into the clear blue sky

our aging parents

over the rainbow

throughout his long life

along our rugged coastline

of justice

beyond the far horizon

John's best album

Story 1:
Under the powerful hoist in the hot shed the bush mechanic was giving life back to the very dead car. By the open door near the overhanging branch of the pepper tree the owners waited.

Story 2:
The aging trees had an icy wind in their long branches.

The cracked road had twigs and small stones on its surface.

The unhappy group of miserable pigs was a cold collection of woeful weary animals.

The Preposition Exercise Answers

Your first strategy is to box the nouns. Secondly, identify the prepositional phrases. Thirdly, cross them out and fourthly, within the stories, add the spotlight to the main character.

Words:

into the clear blue sky

our aging parents

over the rainbow

throughout his long life

along our rugged coastline

of justice

beyond the far horizon

John's best album

Story 1:

Under the powerful hoist in the hot shed the bush mechanic was giving life back to the very dead car. By the open door near the overhanging branch of the pepper tree the owners waited.

Story 2:

The aging trees had an icy wind in their long branches. The cracked road had twigs and small stones on its surface. The unhappy group of miserable pigs was a cold collection of woeful weary animals.

PICTURE 7: The Verb

> **Verbs have families.**

Like the referee, verbs direct the main character (or players) within a sentence.

For simplicity the Picture can be drawn without the face.

The farmers have cows.

The pigs have a messy kitchen.

The Verb Strategy:

Make sure to always draw it through the word: a little above and a little below and with a straight back. Always draw it with a straight back.

The Verb in Use

Every verb has a family of words. These are called the conjugations of the verb. Words from the verb are especially chosen to match with the main character.

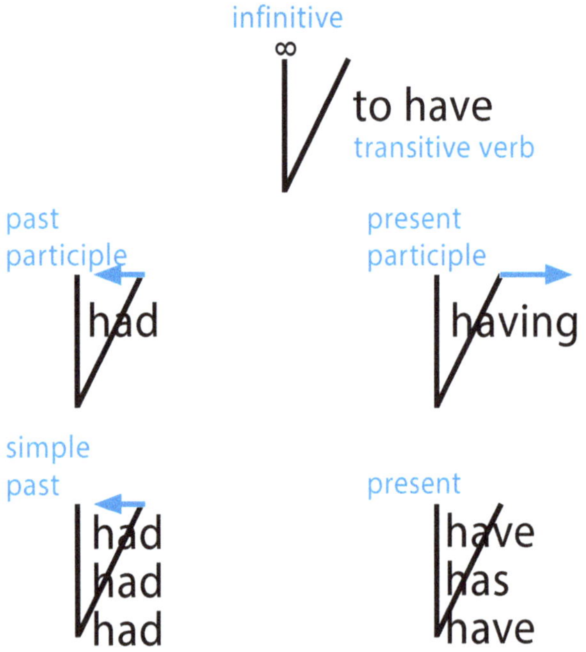

infinitive
∞
to have
transitive verb

past participle
had

present participle
having

— One verb and 4 family members

*Four ways to match with a main character.

simple past
had
had
had

present
have
has
have

infinitive
∞
to be
linking verb

past participle
been

present participle
being

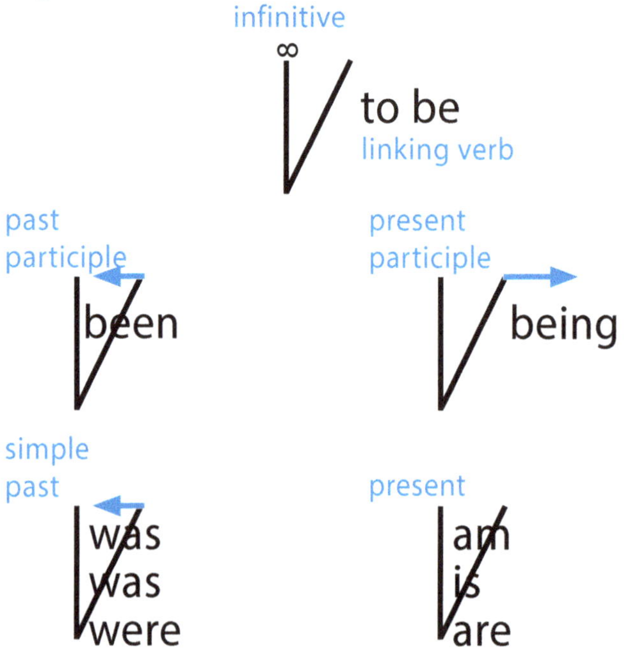

One verb and 8 family members

*Eight ways to match with a main character.
(And!!! this verb is used more than any other).

simple past
was
was
were

present
am
is
are

PAGE 38

The Verb Exercise

In the words (first section), draw the picture through a possible verb. In the sentences (second and third sections), always begin by boxing the nouns, growing the shadow to the determiner, understanding that the noun phrase may be the object of the preposition (cut that prepositional phrase out).

Words:

had	through	have	been
being	underneath	backpack	people
was	is	are	were
to	during	upon	between

Sentences 1:

The pigs had a troubled life. The farmer has a brilliant wife.

My aunty has a good friend in another suburb across the city.

At home in the kitchen Mum has new benchtops.

Sentences 2:

Under a summer sky the cows were happy in their paddocks.

Cheetahs are wonderful biological machines of amazing speed.

The zebra is cautious. The queen was a woman of wisdom.

The Verb Exercise Answers

#7 In the words section, draw the picture through a possible verb. In the sentences sections, always begin by boxing the nouns, growing the shadow to the determiner, understanding that the noun phrase may be the object of the preposition cut that prepositional phrase out. Make

Words:

~~had~~	through	~~have~~	~~been~~
~~being~~	underneath	backpack	people
~~was~~	~~is~~	~~are~~	~~were~~
to	during	upon	between

Sentences 1:

The pigs had a troubled life. The farmer has a brilliant wife.

My aunty has a good friend in another suburb across the city.

At home in the kitchen Mum has new benchtops.

Sentences 2:

Under a summer sky the cows were happy in their paddocks.

Cheetahs are wonderful biological machines of amazing speed.

The zebra is cautious. The queen was a woman of wisdom.

PICTURE 8a: The Adverb with Adjectives

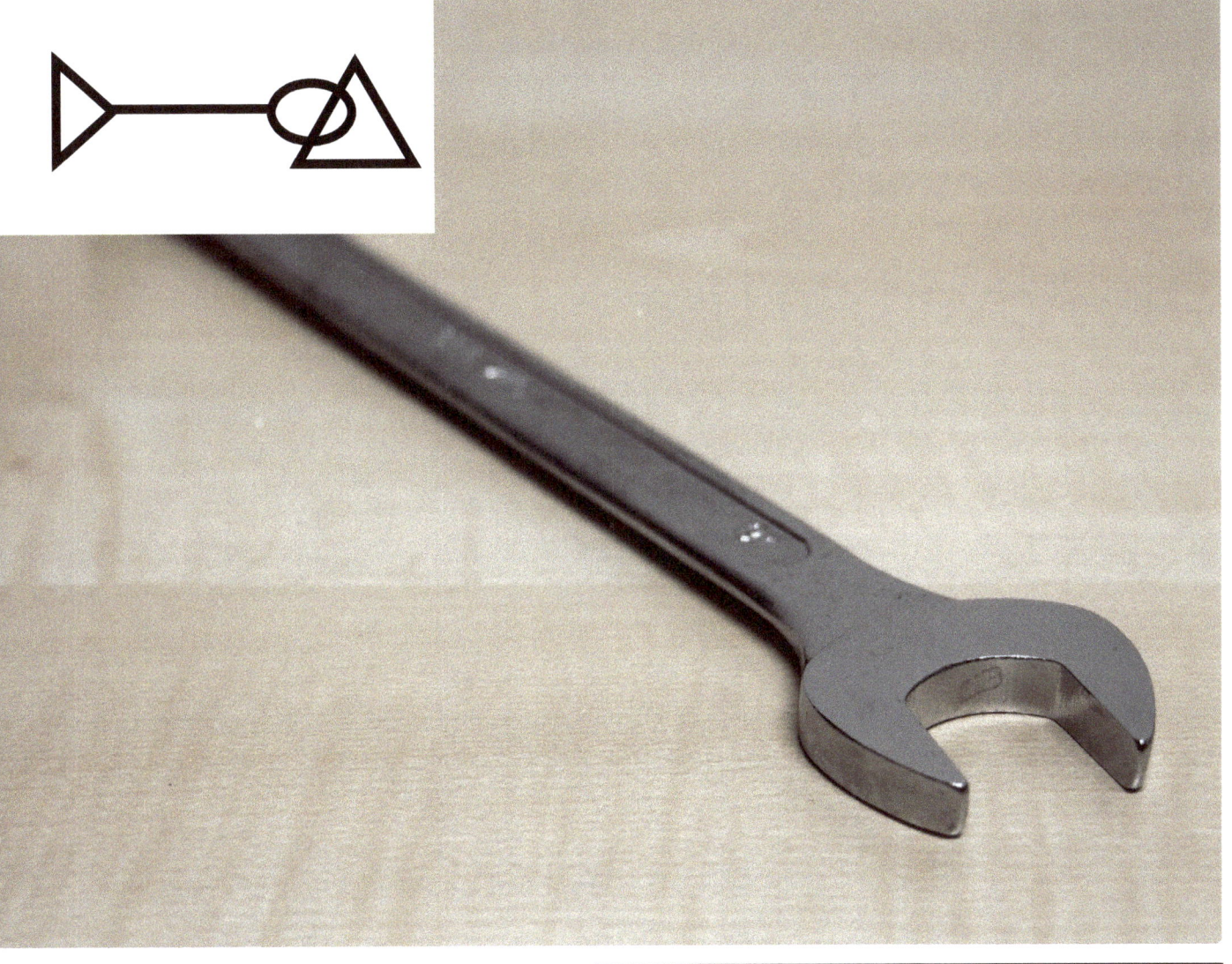

Lots of adverbs are made by adding ly (a suffix) to the end of an adjective.

"When the adverb has a handle on an adjective, it can be an intensifier such as very or really."

The Adverb Strategy:

To draw the picture for an adverb it is simply a triangle (the handle), beginning at the adverb, connecting to the adjective with an oval.

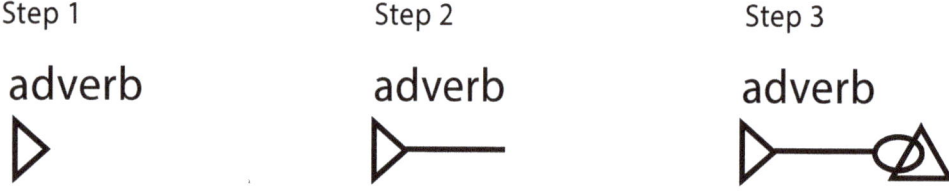

Step 1

Step 2

Step 3

The Adverb In Use:

Turning an adjective into an adverb is easy. Lots of adverbs are made by adding ly (a suffix) to the end of an adjective.

Adjectives	Adverbs
accurate	accurately
bad	badly
certain	certainly
different	differently
easy	easily
free	freely

The adverb and the adjective are linked. Having a handle on an adjective can turn its volume up or down. Adverbs handling adjectives are called intensifiers: they are clearly associated with the adjective not the verb.

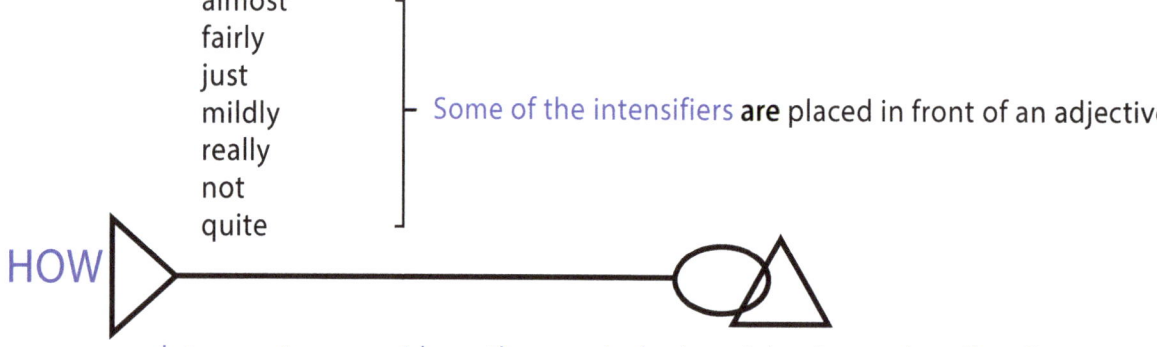

almost
fairly
just
mildly
really
not
quite

Some of the intensifiers **are** placed in front of an adjective.

HOW

Adjectives can complete a sentence or ride on the noun's shadow. Adverbs can handle adjectives wherever they are.

Adverb Examples:

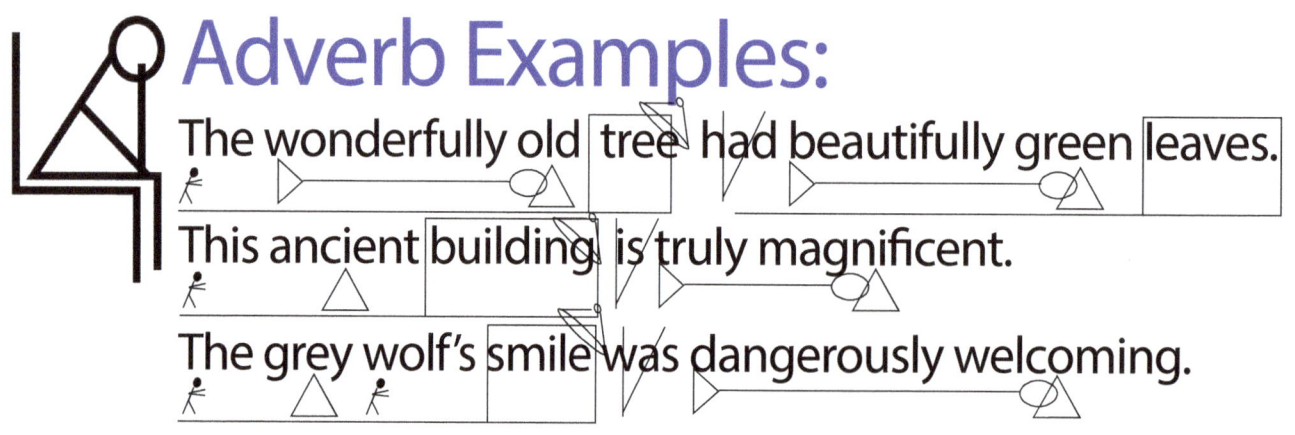

The wonderfully old tree had beautifully green leaves.

This ancient building is truly magnificent.

The grey wolf's smile was dangerously welcoming.

PAGE 42

The Adverb Exercise

Transform the adjectives into adverbs, by adding the ly (suffix).

Convert:

Adjectives	Adverbs
absolute	absolute___
amazing	amazing___
complete	complete___
incredible	incredib___
real	real___
terrible	terrib___
total	total___
utter	utter___

Always begin by decluttering the sentence: boxing the nouns, growing the shadow appropriately, showing adjectives, cutting out prepositional phrases, drawing in the verb (with a straight back). Now draw the adverbs handling the adjectives.

Story 1:

Our mainly small team had a surprisingly good win over the Giants. For a small boat the exceptionally wide river was truly dangerous. That wholly charming Isaac is enormously rich in his many talents.

The Adverb Exercise Answers

Form the adjectives into adverbs, by adding the ly (suffix)

Convert:

Adjectives	Adverbs	
absolute	absolutely	
amazing	amazingly	
complete	completely	
incredible	incredibly	note slight change in pattern
real	really	
terrible	terribly	note slight change in pattern
total	totally	
utter	utterly	

Always begin by decluttering the sentence: boxing the nouns, growing the shadow appropriately, showing adjectives, cutting out prepositional phrases, drawing in the verb (with a straight back). Now draw the adverbs handling the adjectives.

Story 1:

Our mainly small team had a surprisingly good win over the Giants. For a small boat the exceptionally wide river was truly dangerous. That wholly charming Isaac is enormously rich in his many talents.

PICTURE 8b: The Adverb with Verbs

Adverbs when connected to a verb have the ability to make even clearer the directions in the sentence.

" When the adverb has a handle on a verb, it's giving information about how, when, where or why. "

The Adverb in Use With Verbs

Adverbs can go either side of the verb

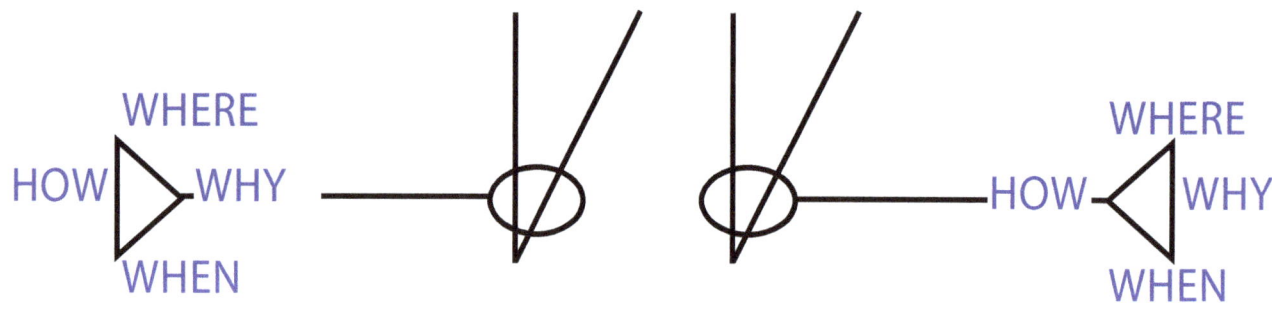

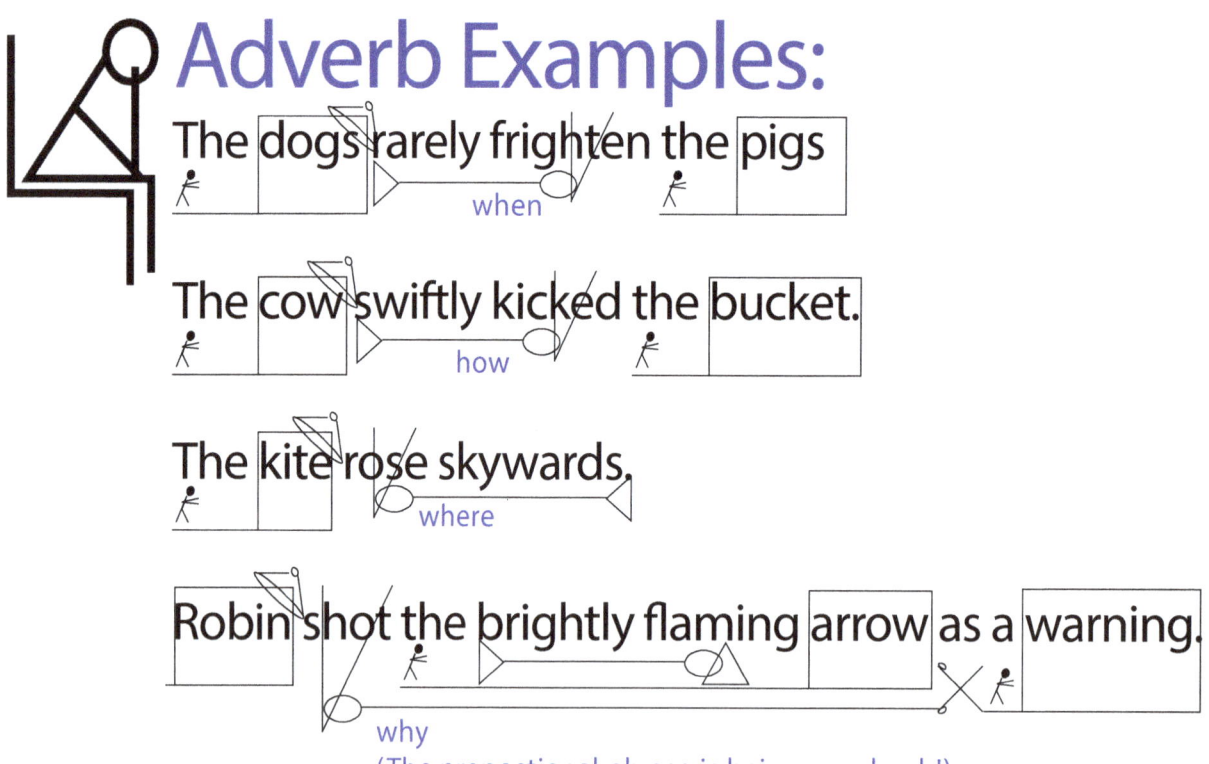

Adverb Examples:

The dogs rarely frighten the pigs
when

The cow swiftly kicked the bucket.
how

The kite rose skywards.
where

Robin shot the brightly flaming arrow as a warning.
why
(The prepostional phrase is being an adverb!)

The Adverb Exercise

Adverbs handling a verb will tell how, where, when or why (often a prepositional phrase).

Always begin by decluttering the sentence: boxing the nouns, growing the shadow appropriately, showing adjectives, cutting out prepositional phrases, and then drawing in the verb (with a straight back). Now draw the adverbs handling verbs.

Story 1:

The heavy statues in the lush garden always had a blanket of shade. During the late afternoon a gardener secretly has a refreshing drink behind his back. The children scattered the leaves randomly.

A new story to work on. Adverbs must connect to either an adjective or a verb.

Story 2:

Tragically poor Cinderella lived economically in a cold drafty house. Cinderella unhappily shared the truly awful cottage with her dreadful stepmother and two unbelievably selfish stepsisters. In all circumstances from the very bleak dawn until the depressingly dreary evenings Cinderella cleaned the horrid house. With complete attention to every detail Cinderella silently worked.

The Adverb Exercise Answers

Adverbs handling a verb will tell how, where, when or why (often a prepositional phrase).

Always begin by decluttering the sentence: boxing the nouns, growing the shadow appropriately, showing adjectives, cutting out prepositional phrases, and then drawing in the verb (with a straight back). Now draw the adverbs handling verbs.

Story 1:

The heavy statues in the lush garden always had a blanket of shade. During the late afternoon a gardener secretly has a refreshing drink behind his back. The children scattered the leaves randomly.

A new story to work on. Adverbs must connect to either an adjective or a verb.

Story 2:

Tragically poor Cinderella lived economically in a cold drafty house. Cinderella unhappily shared the truly awful cottage with her dreadful stepmother and two unbelievably selfish stepsisters. In all circumstances from the very bleak dawn until the depressingly dreary evenings Cinderella cleaned the horrid house. With complete attention to every detail Cinderella silently worked.

PICTURE 9: The Conjunction

> **The most famous conjunction is "and"**

It's elementary! Conjunctions see similar elements in a sentence and are able to bring them together:

                nouns with nouns
                verbs with verbs
           adjectives with adjectives
 prepositional phrases with prepositional phrases

example

I like netball and hockey.

Monica ran and jumped all over the court.

Those cars are black and white.

We ran down the sandhills and onto the beach.

Types of Conjunctions

And with fame, comes the fans! In fact FANBOYS! (The beginning letter of each word.)

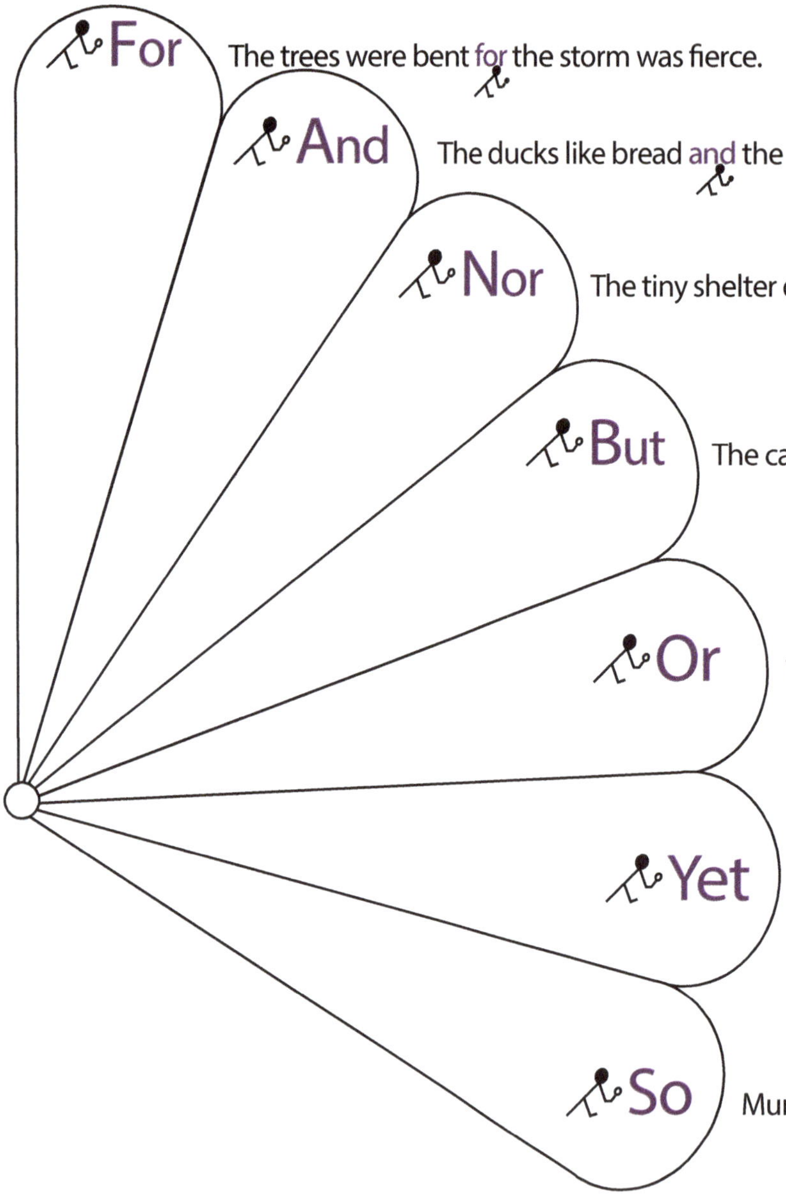

For — The trees were bent for the storm was fierce.

And — The ducks like bread and the monkeys like fruit.

Nor — The tiny shelter did not cool the tribe nor ease their worry.

But — The carpenter worked easily but the helper struggled.

Or — The match could be won or lost.

Yet — Sam was scared yet she loved to play in the tunnels.

So — Mum fixed the puncture so Paul could ride the bike.

These 7 conjunctions are used to indicate an "equal value" of information in each of the connected sentences. This "equal value" of information means that each clause has a main character, and the sentence itself will have 2 spotlights. Furthermore, when analysing a sentence, these special conjunctions belong to neither piece of information (they are connectors).

Conjunction Examples:

A compound sentence is the:
  joining of two clauses   with   a coordinating conjunction.

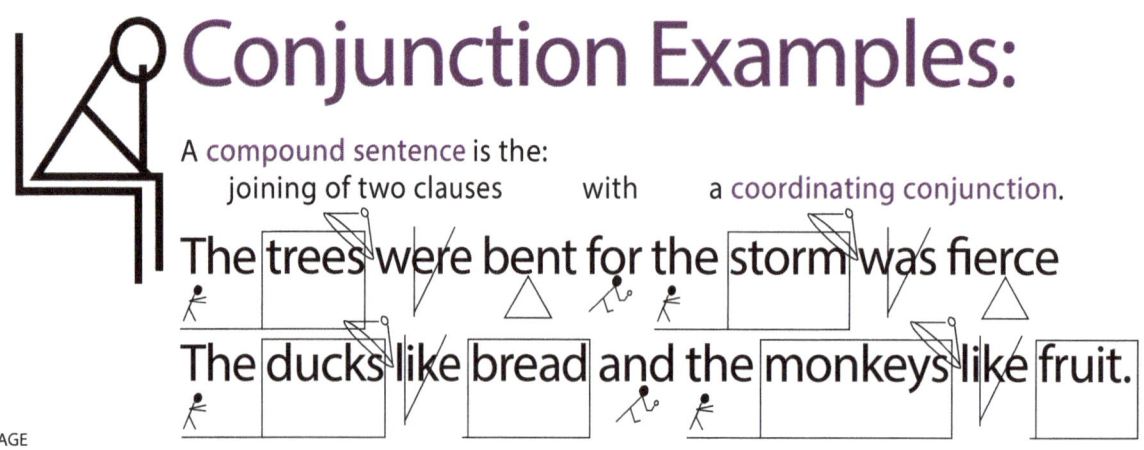

PAGE 50

Conjunctions Exercise Part 1

Getting comfortable with more than just one verb in a sentence, still using the family members from "to have" and "to be" (page 38).

These sentences are in pairs.
             They will be joined later.

Step 1: Always begin by decluttering the sentence: boxing the nouns, growing the shadow appropriately, showing adjectives, cutting out prepositional phrases.

Drawing in the verb (with a straight back) is the focus, because we want to create a sentence with two verbs, and possibly two spotlights.
(Any adverbs? Not always. When used, adverbs handle an adjective or verb)

Sentences

The trees had no leaves.	The season was autumn.
The waves were choppy.	The fierce wind had a dangerous edge.
The winter sun was not warming.	The cold house having comfort*
The Tasmanian Devil was cute.	The shrieking monkey had the crowd's attention.
Jo had summer holidays in Wales.	Jo had summer holidays in Italy.
Trent was a wonderful player.	The team always had Toni in the centre.
The team's colours are similar.	The visiting team has black shorts.

* Note: "The cold house having comfort" is not a sentence. It does not have a complete verb, but only a main character followed by a participle phrase. Using a complete verb, the sentence could read: The cold house had comfort.

Conjunctions Ex. Part 1 Answers

Getting comfortable with more than just one verb in a sentence, still using the family members from "to have" and "to be" (page 38).

These sentences are in pairs.
                 They will be joined later.

Step 1: Always begin by decluttering the sentence: boxing the nouns, growing the shadow appropriately, showing adjectives, cutting out prepositional phrases.

Drawing in the verb (with a straight back) is the focus, because we want to create a sentence with two verbs, and possibly two spotlights.
(Any adverbs? Not always. When used, adverbs handle an adjective or verb)

Sentences

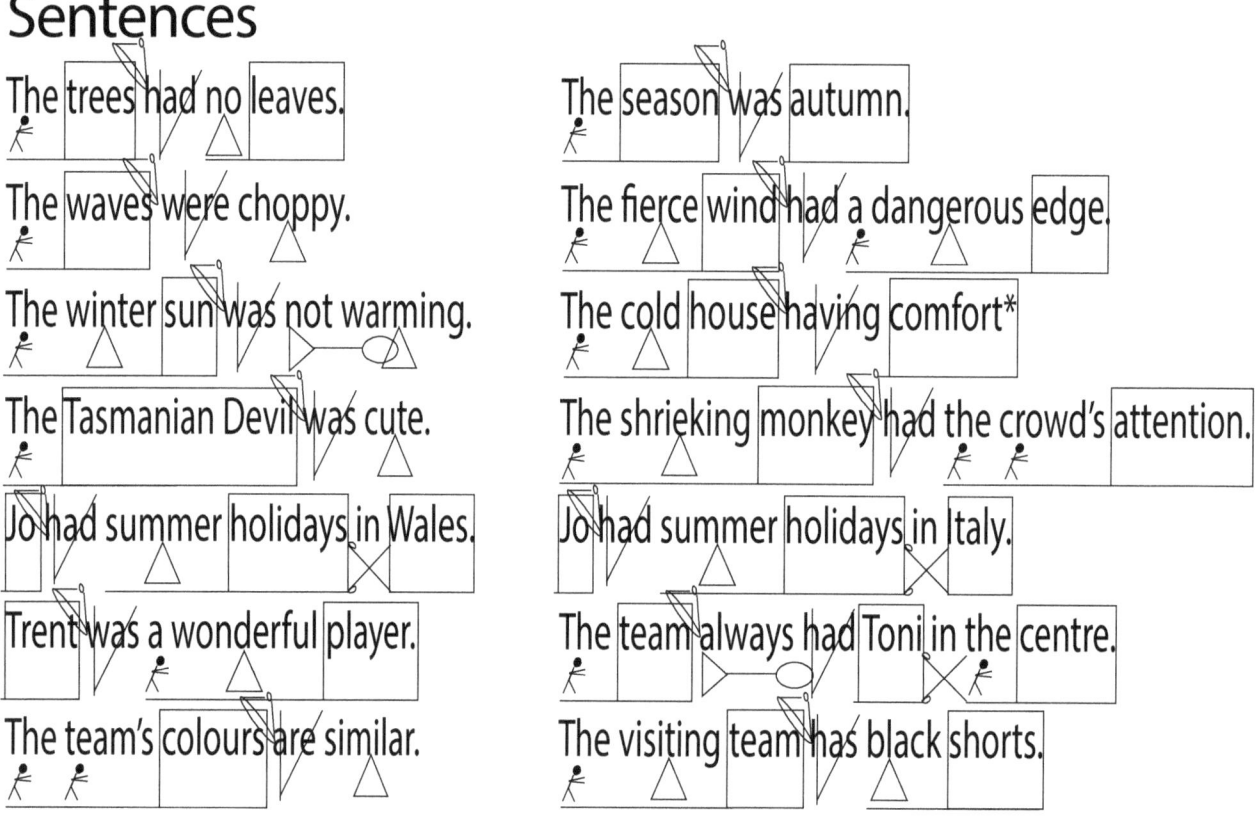

* Note: "The cold house having comfort" is not a sentence. It does not have a complete verb, but only a main character followed by a participle phrase. Using a complete verb, the sentence could read: The cold house had comfort.

Conjunctions Exercise Part 2

Join the sentence pairs to create one very much longer sentence. Use the suggested conjunction. Replace the capital letter at the beginning of the second sentence (the fullstop has been removed from the first clause).

Sentences

The trees had no leaves   f__ _he season was autumn.

The waves were choppy   a__ _he fierce wind had a dangerous edge.

The winter sun was not warming   n__ _he cold house having comfort.

The Tasmanian Devil was cute   b__ _he shrieking monkey had the crowd's attention.

Jo had summer holidays in Wales o_   Jo had summer holidays in Italy.

Trent was a wonderful player   y__ _he team always had Toni in the centre.

The team's colours are similar   s_   _he visiting team has black shorts.

Story 1:

The disengagingly ugly sisters were mean to Cinderella for Cinderella was engagingly pretty. The sisters cruelly pinched Cinderella and the sisters painfully poked Cinderella. Cinderella was too slow with her tiresomely humdrum household tasks. Cinderella had no hope of friendship nor the opportunity of peace within the household.

Conjunctions Ex. Part 2 Answers

Join the sentence pairs to create one very much longer sentence. Use the suggested conjunction. Replace the capital letter at the beginning of the second sentence (the fullstop has been removed from the first clause).

Sentences

The trees had no leaves	for	the season was autumn.
The waves were choppy	and	the fierce wind had a dangerous edge.
The winter sun was not warming	nor	the cold house having comfort.
The Tasmanian Devil was cute	but	the shrieking monkey had the crowd's attention.
Jo had summer holidays in Wales	or	Jo had summer holidays in Italy.
Trent was a wonderful player	yet	the team always had Toni in the centre.
The team's colours are similar	so	the visiting team has black shorts.

Story 1:

The disengagingly ugly sisters were mean to Cinderella for Cinderella was engagingly pretty. The sisters cruelly pinched Cinderella and the sisters painfully poked Cinderella. Cinderella was too slow with her tiresomely humdrum household tasks. Cinderella had no hope of friendship nor the opportunity of peace within the household.

PICTURE 10: The Relative Pronoun & Its Clause

> **"** The **relative pronoun** always appears **straight after the noun** and is **related to that noun**. **"**

The relative pronoun is cut out of the noun creating the triangular shape of the adjective

which is used to add detail about an animal or a thing.
who is used to add detail about a person.

Like an adjective the relative pronoun clause adds detail about a noun. This detail could be removed.

that is used to add essential (non-removable) information for the reader.

The Relative Pronoun Strategy:

Remembering you have already boxed the nouns, draw the picture as shown making sure the picture stretches lower than the noun phrase because it's going to contain the nouns that have already been boxed.

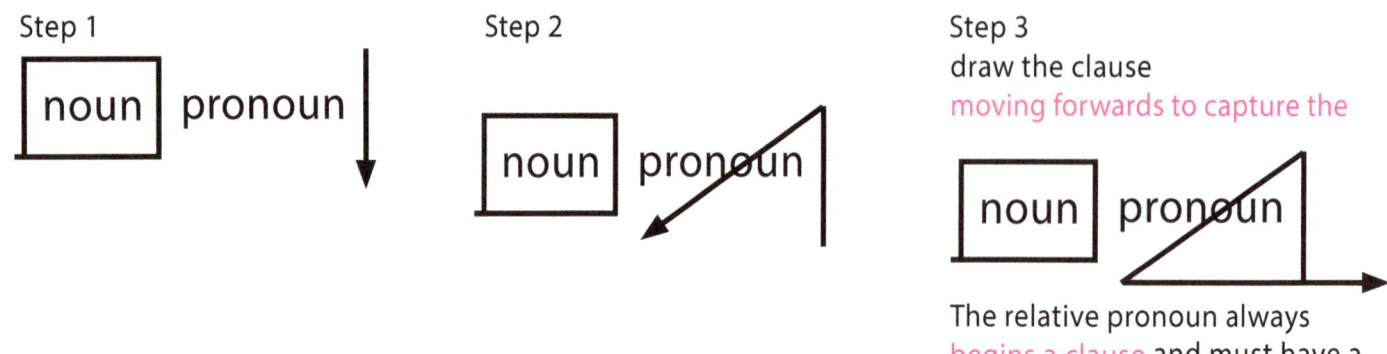

The relative pronoun always begins a clause and must have a verb. It creates complex sentences.

The Relative Pronoun Examples:

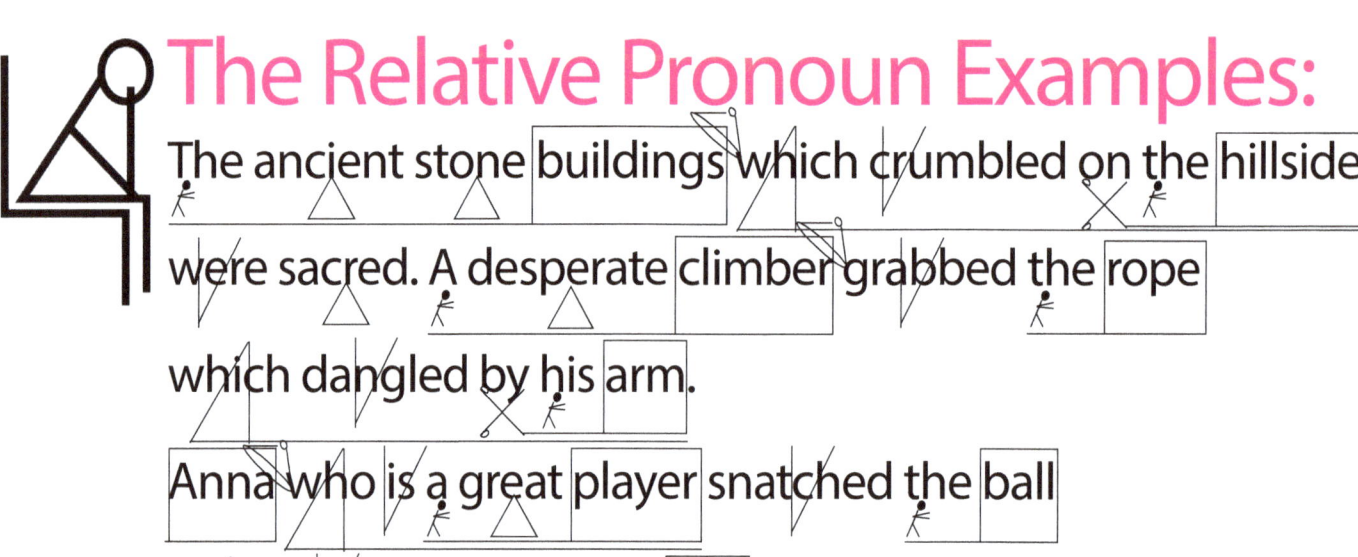

The ancient stone buildings which crumbled on the hillside were sacred. A desperate climber grabbed the rope which dangled by his arm.

Anna who is a great player snatched the ball which bounced near the line.

Mr Clause who was so famous for his work with chimneys hit the roof.

Below, "that" is used to create essential detail that can't be removed: it's called a restrictive clause. Not every apple is poisonous, only the stranger's.

The apples that the stranger offered were poisonous.

Note: The added clause is really a mini-sentence. It has a main character (the relative pronoun) and a verb.

Relative Pronoun Exercise

Most of the decluttering has been done. Draw in the relative pronoun clauses. Begin with the relative pronoun, and then move forward to include the verb and other elements.

Sentences:

The spirited horse which kicked down the barn door was usually troublesome.

My old truck that blows horrible smoke is a monster which is an embarrassment to the family.

Chloe who was nearly eleven gave Gemma a cake which was simply enormous.

Cinderella continues with conjunctions and relative pronoun clauses. Box the nouns first.

Story 1:

The mice which scampered around the dark and dingy house absolutely loved Cinderella. These adoring mice were small but her truly delightful companions. Cinderella who was always kind left small yet tasty scraps which were well toasted by the fire.

Relative Pronoun Exercise Answers

#10 Most of the decluttering has been done. Draw in the relative pronoun clauses. Begin with the relative pronoun, and then move forward to include the verb and other elements.

Sentences:

The spirited horse which kicked down the barn door was usually troublesome.

My old truck that blows horrible smoke is a monster which is an embarrassment to the family.

Chloe who was nearly eleven gave Gemma a cake which was simply enormous.

Cinderella continues with conjunctions and relative pronoun clauses. Box the nouns first.

Story 1:

The mice which scampered around the dark and dingy house absolutely loved Cinderella. These adoring mice were small but her truly delightful companions. Cinderella who was always kind left small yet tasty scraps which were well toasted by the fire.

ADDITIONAL EXERCISES

Keep connecting with the pictures. Keep practising the patterns.

> " Exercises can strengthen the mind. "

Additional Exercise (1)

Match the words with the images to create structured sentences. All of the verbs come from "to be" and "to have".

lunch child a hungry delicious The had

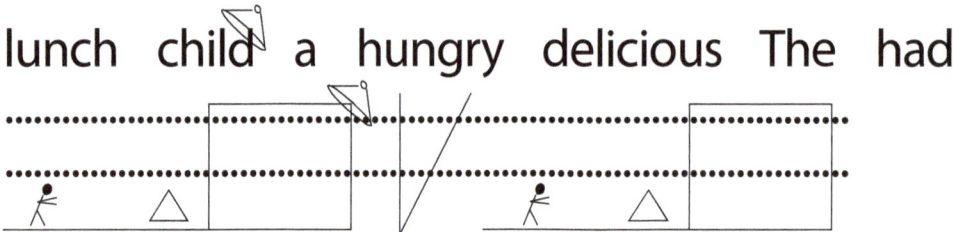

active Those some on had exercise students oval the

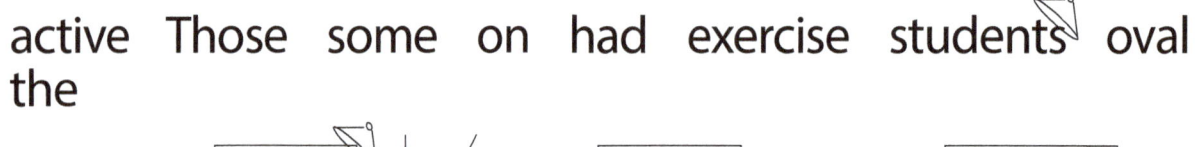

always nap afternoon In the late a has Nanna

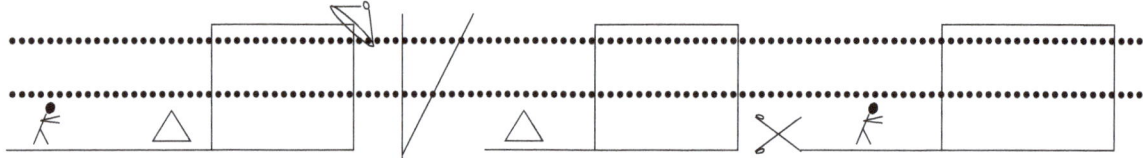

peaches with absolutely The skin soft fuzzy were mouth-watering

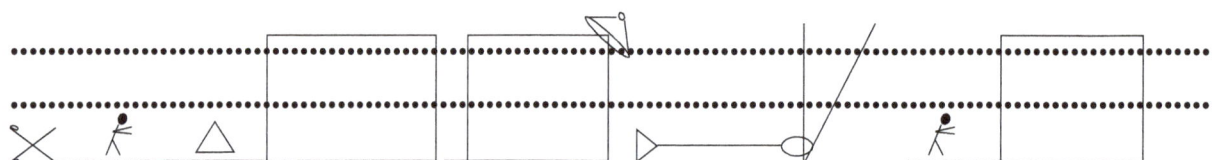

Additional Exercise (2)

Match the words with the images to create structured sentences. All of the verbs come from "to be" and "to have".

notably animals no Jo's parents yet good had were pets with Jo

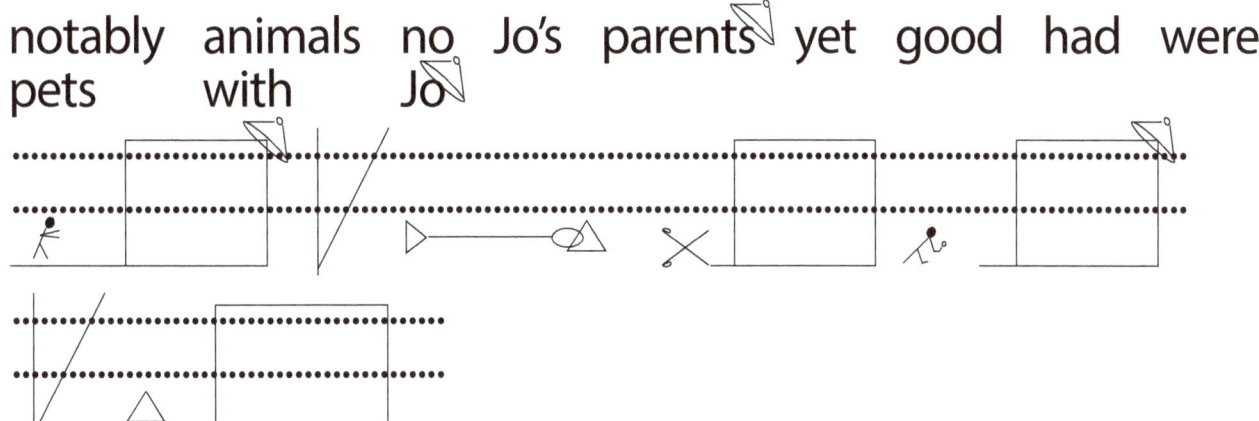

green once The which leaves are an were mess untidy fallen now

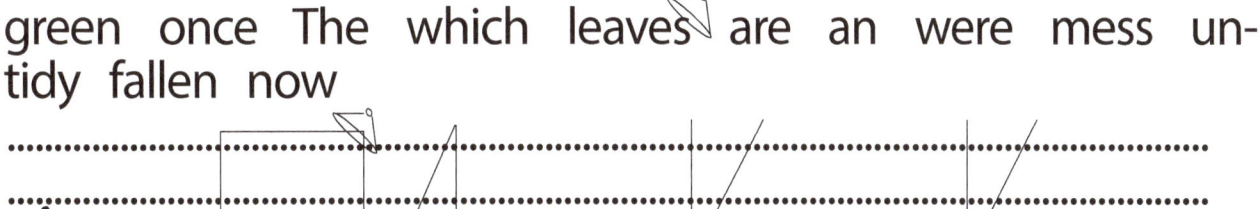

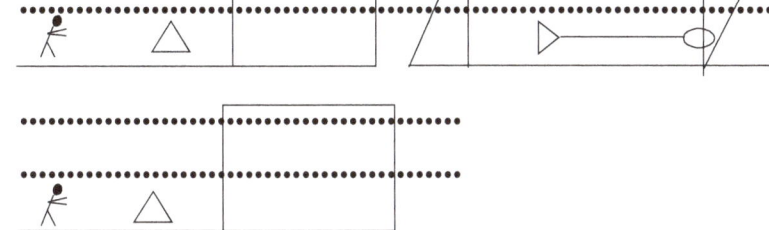

completely who best fearless captain Joe the was choice was for

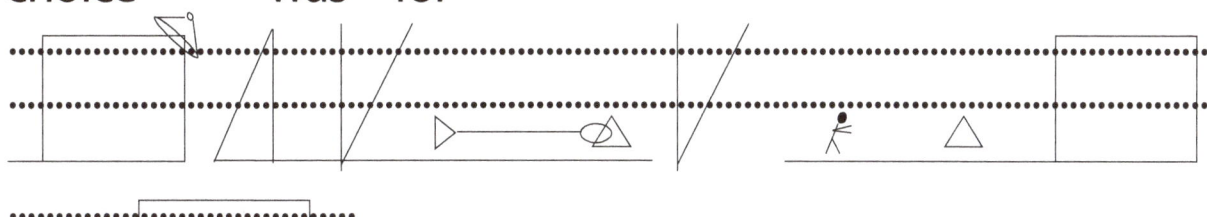

Additional Exercise (1) Answers

Match the words with the images to create structured sentences. All of the verbs come from "to be" and "to have".

lunch child a hungry delicious The had

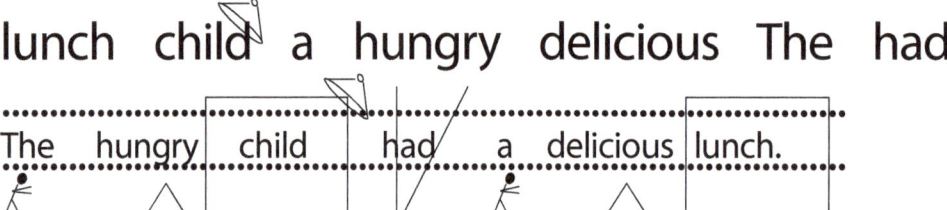

active Those some on had exercise students oval the

always nap afternoon In the late a has Nanna

peaches with absolutely The skin soft fuzzy were mouth-watering

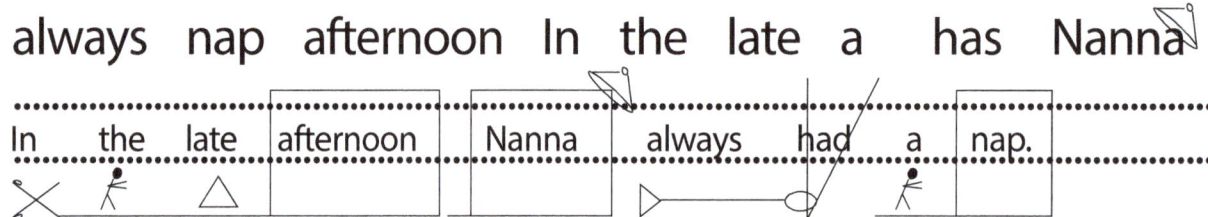

Additional Exercise (2) Answers

Match the words with the images to create structured sentences. All of the verbs come from "to be" and "to have".

notably animals no Jo's parents yet good had were pets with Jo

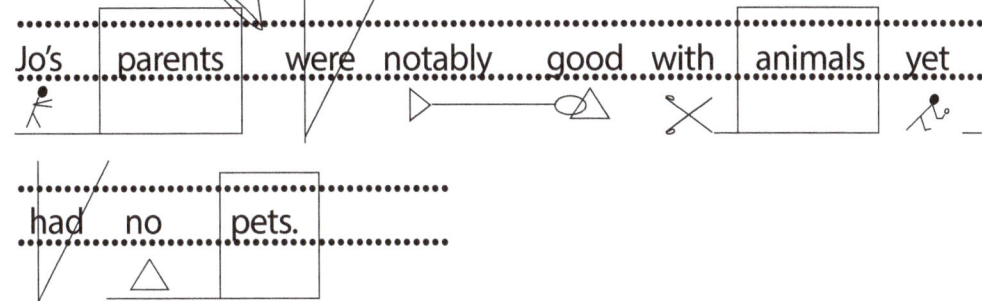

green once The which leaves are an were mess untidy fallen now

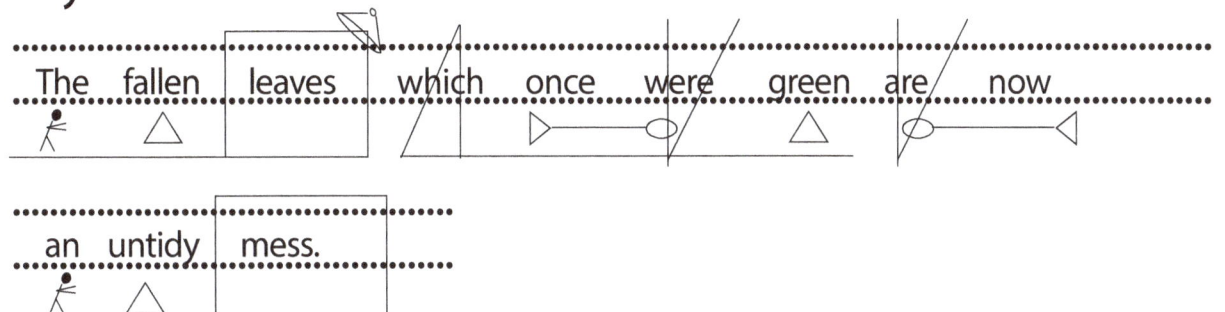

completely who best fearless captain Joe the was choice was for

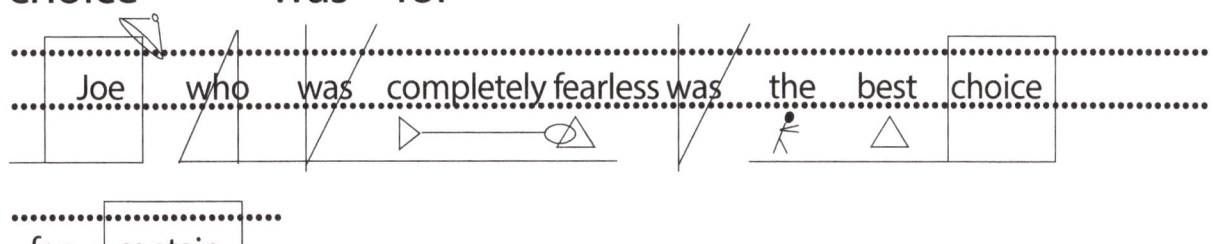

Additional Exercise (3)

Match the words with the images to create structured sentences. All of the verbs come from "to be" and "to have".

brief a game hazard The unusually rain for the sudden was was

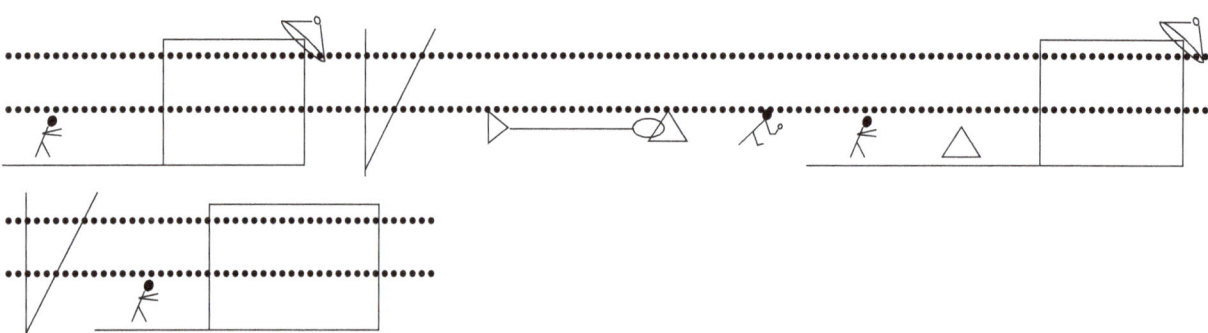

day sweet with Hot on very toast welcome is tea dreary

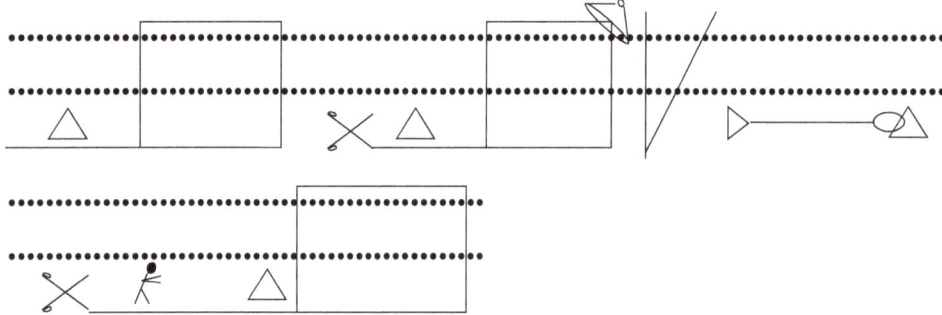

At stars lovely but of always sea eerie is the night are our

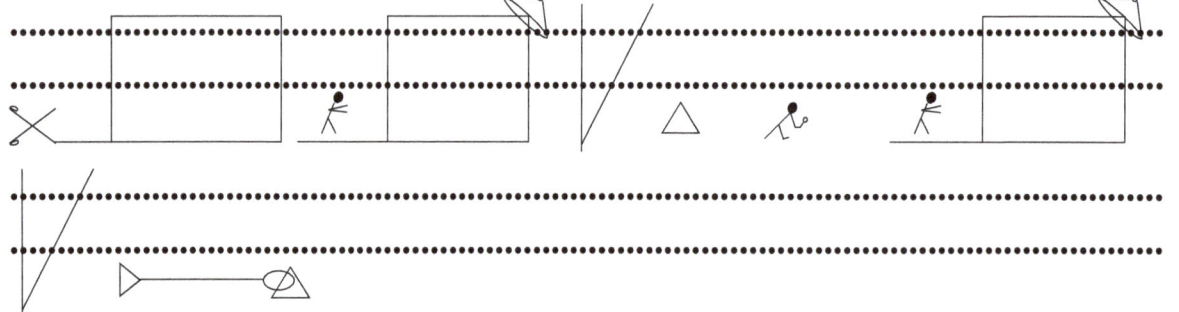

Additional Exercise (4)

PICTURE FIND: Use your creativity and fill in the blanks. Use the images to create the complete sentence.

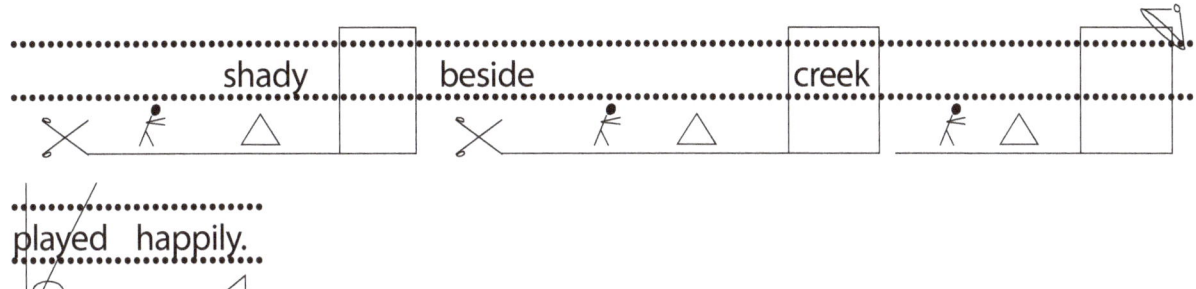

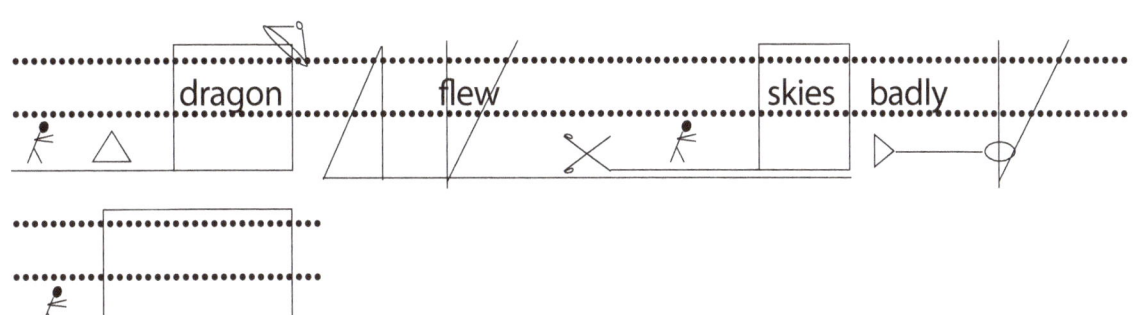

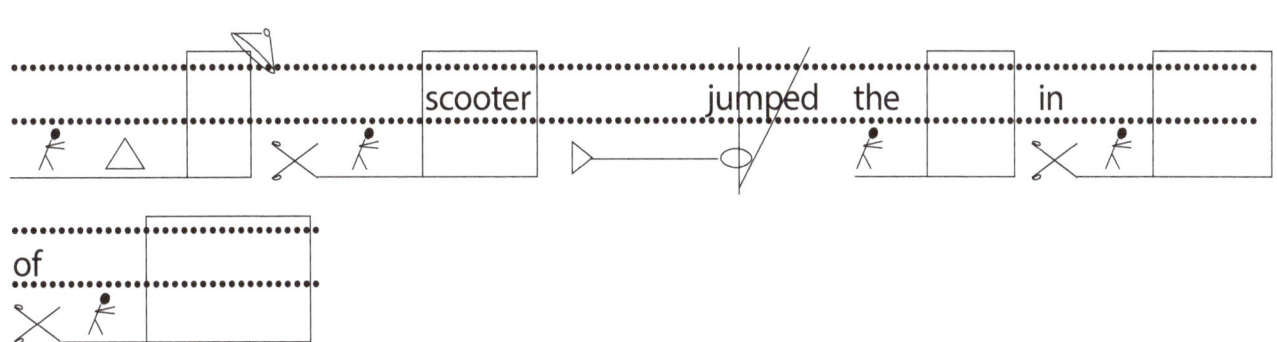

Additional Exercise (3) Answers

Match the words with the images to create structured sentences. All of the verbs come from "to be" and "to have".

brief a game hazard The unusually rain for the sudden was was

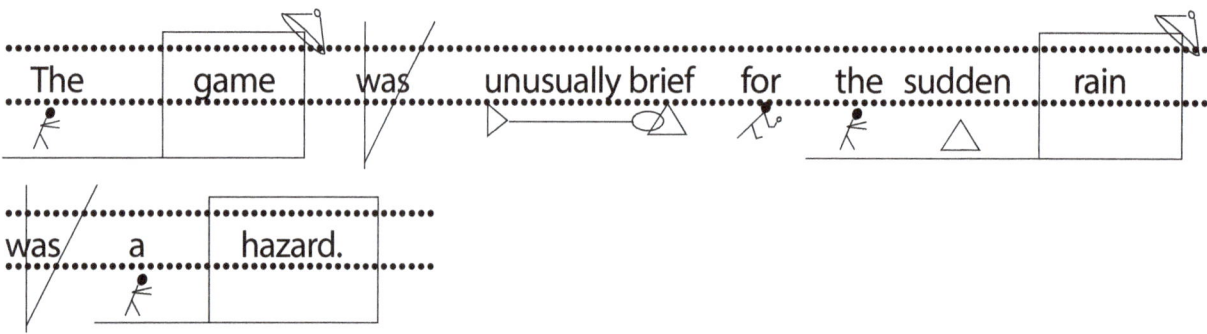

day sweet with Hot on very toast welcome is tea dreary

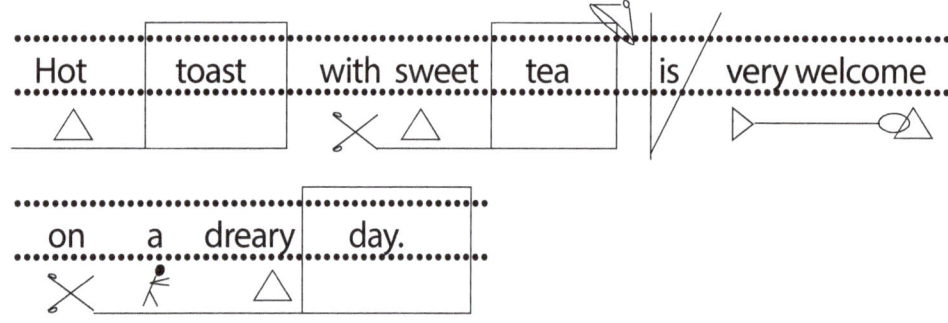

At stars lovely but of always sea eerie is the night are our

Additional Exercise (4) Answers

PICTURE FIND: Use your creativity and fill in the blanks. Use the images to create the complete sentence. Below are possible answers to the exercise.

The crazy monkey in the cage threw stale bananas at the crowd.

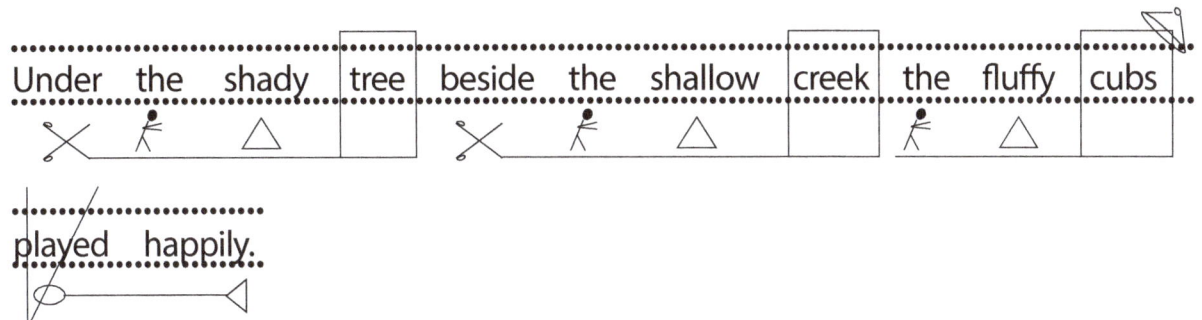

Under the shady tree beside the shallow creek the fluffy cubs played happily.

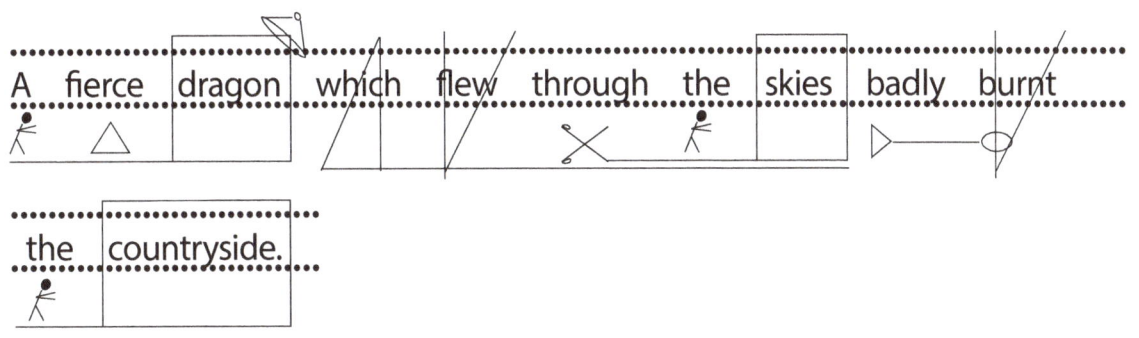

A fierce dragon which flew through the skies badly burnt the countryside.

The little kid on her scooter cleverly jumped the ditch in the middle of the footpath.

GRAMMAR Made Easy

Additional Exercise (5)

SEEK & DRAW: Find the structure, draw the picture.

1. Under the shade of the pepper trees beside the well-worn track

2. stood the sheering sheds, a favourite spot for a family picnic.

3. They hastily loaded the car, mum and dad in the cabin,

4. the kids safely perched in the tray with Dusty, the best dog

5. in the whole wide world. The day was glorious with wisps

6. of white clouds in a perfectly blue sky. Like the back of his hands

7. dad knew the track and easily found the smoothest course

8. through the maze of ruts and the bumps of the uneven surface.

9. Sunlight reflected brilliantly from the iron sheets which were the sides

10. of the shed but the pepper trees cast a deep shade.

11. Dad parked beneath the trees, Dusty easily made the jump and

12. a lovely long lazy afternoon stretched ahead.

Additional Exercise (5) Cont.

Seek List:

Line 1. three prepositional phrases

Line 2. one prepositional phrase

Line 3. verb handled by an adverb, one prepositional phrase

Line 4. verb handled by an adverb, two prepositional phrases

Line 5. two prepositional phrases

Line 6. four prepositional phrases, an adjective handled by an adverb

Line 7. verb handled by an adverb

Line 8. three prepositional phrases

Line 9. verb handled by an adverb, one prepositional phrase, a relative pronoun and the following verb

Line 10. one prepositional phrase, a conjunction

Line 11. one prepositional phrase, a verb handled by an adverb

Line 12. three adjectives riding on the noun's shadow, a verb handled by an adverb.

Additional Exercise (5) Answers

SEEK & DRAW: Find the structure, draw the picture.

1. Under the shade of the pepper trees beside the well-worn track
2. stood the sheering sheds, a favourite spot for a family picnic.
3. They hastily loaded the car, mum and dad in the cabin,
4. the kids safely perched in the tray with Dusty, the best dog
5. in the whole wide world. The day was glorious with wisps
6. of white clouds in a perfectly blue sky. Like the back of his hands
7. dad knew the track and easily found the smoothest course
8. through the maze of ruts and the bumps on the uneven surface.
9. Sunlight reflected brilliantly from the iron sheets which were the sides
10. of the shed but the pepper trees cast a deep shade.
11. Dad parked beneath the trees, Dusty easily made the jump and
12. a lovely long lazy afternoon stretched ahead.

Additional Exercise (5) Cont.

Seek List:

Line 1. three prepositional phrases

Line 2. one prepositional phrase

Line 3. verb handled by an adverb, one prepositional phrase

Line 4. verb handled by an adverb, two prepositional phrases

Line 5. two prepositional phrases

Line 6. four prepositional phrases, an adjective handled by an adverb

Line 7. verb handled by an adverb

Line 8. three prepositional phrases

Line 9. verb handled by an adverb, one prepositional phrase, a relative pronoun and the following verb

Line 10. one prepositional phrase, a conjunction

Line 11. one prepositional phrase, a verb handled by an adverb

Line 12. three adjectives riding on the noun's shadow, a verb handled by an adverb.

Additional Exercise (6)

Match the sentences with the images. Check by adding the text

a. Within the hollow log a colony of insects happily made a safe home.

b. A small insect colony happily made a safe home within the log.

c. The log which was hollow happily made a safe home for the insects.

d.

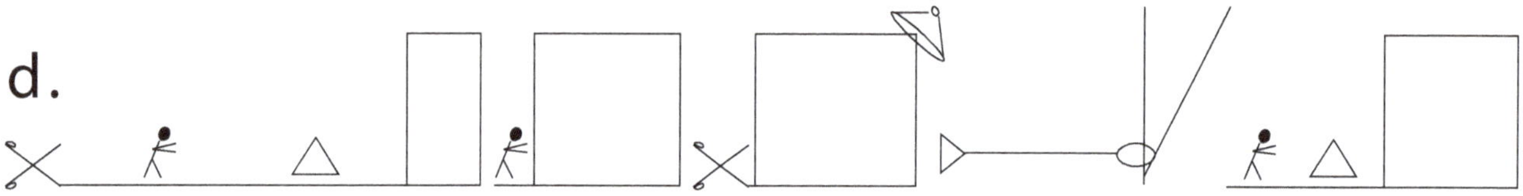

e.

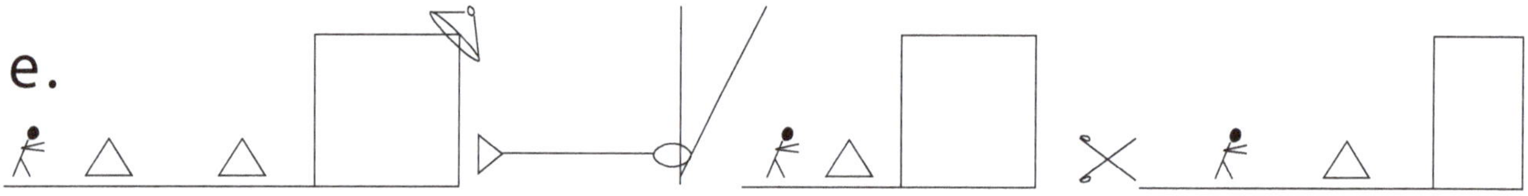

f.

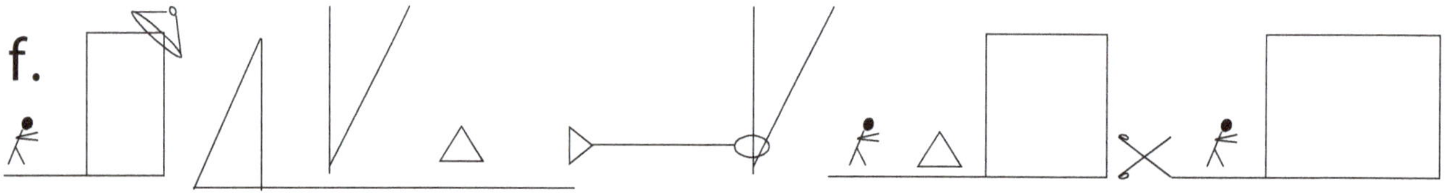

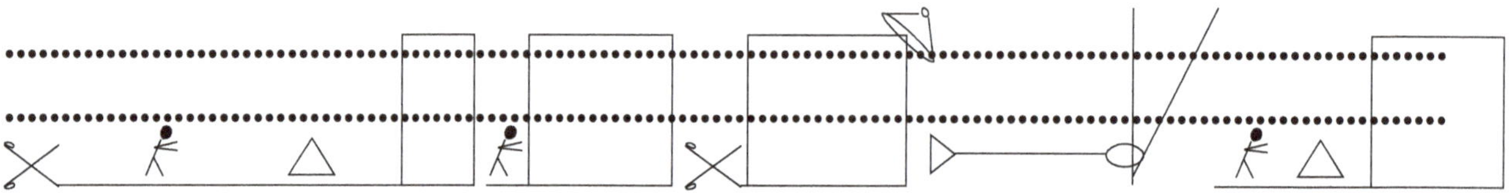

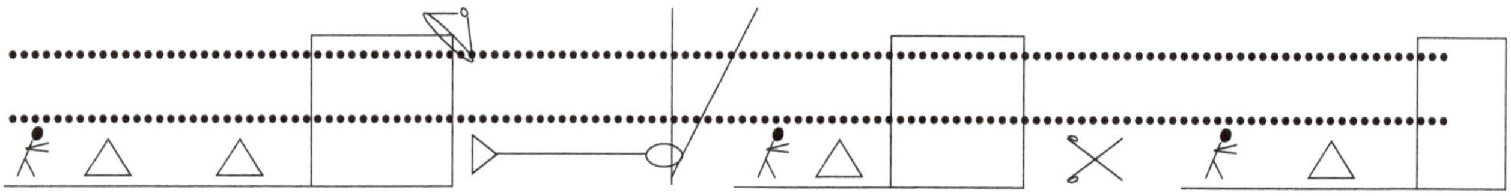

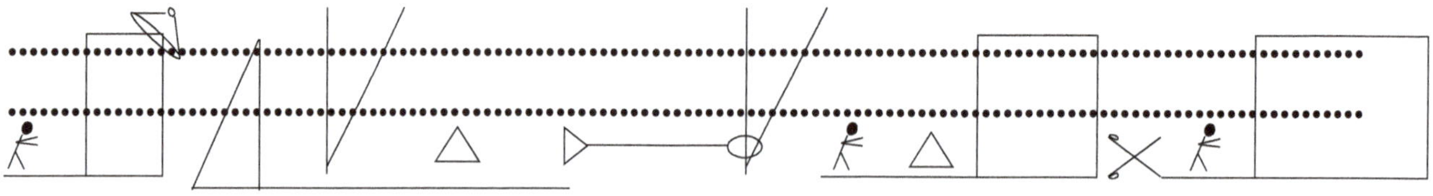

Additional Exercise (7)

Match the sentences with the images. Check by adding the text

a. The famous actor had a soft pleasant face yet her voice was always harsh.

b. The actor who was famous always had a harsh voice but a pleasant face.

c. With a pleasant face the actor was famous and also known for her harshness.

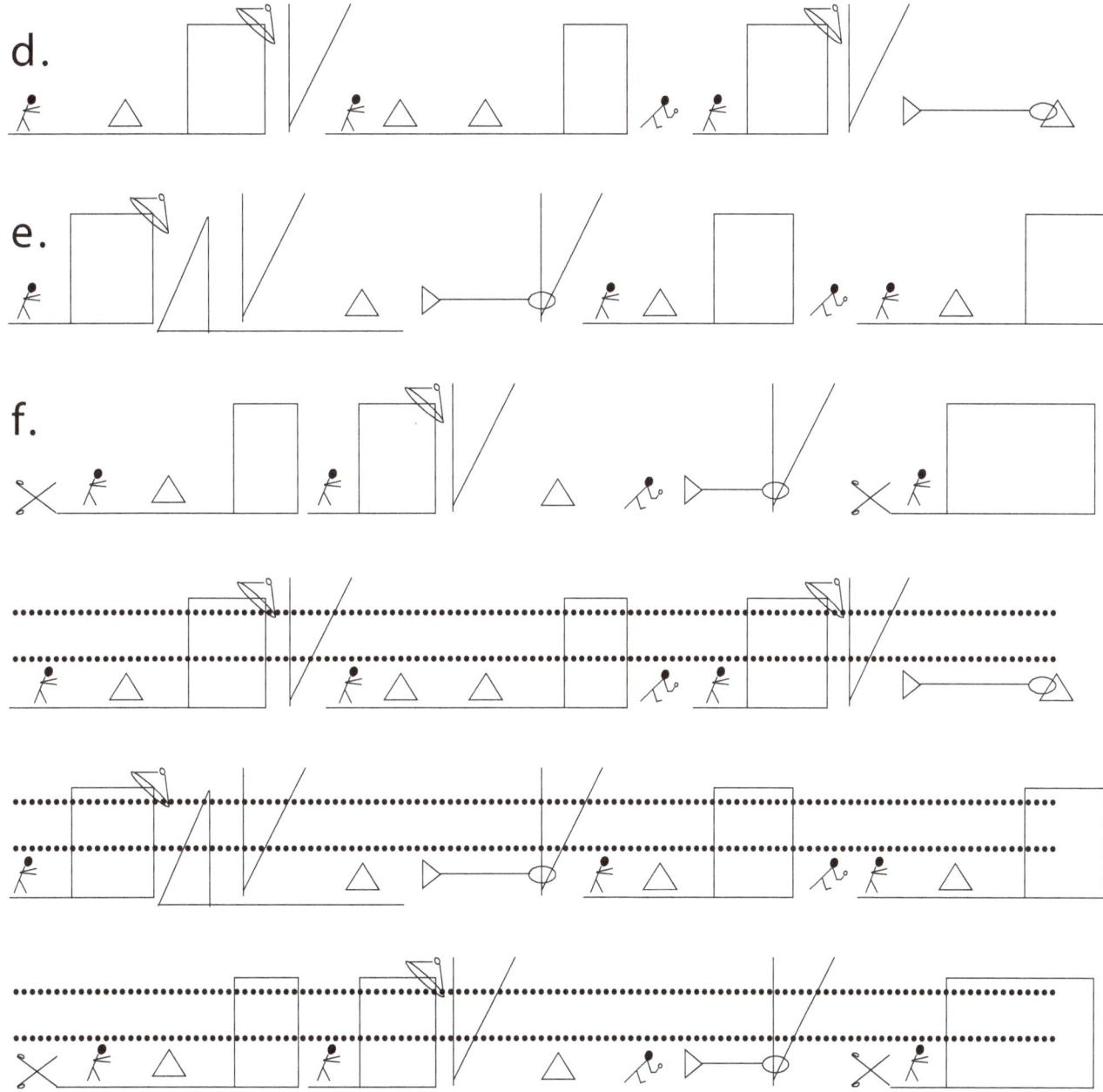

Additional Exercise (6) Answers

Match the sentences with the images. Check by adding the text

a. Within the hollow log a colony of insects happily made a safe home.

b. A small insect colony happily made a safe home within the log.

c. The log which was hollow happily made a safe home for the insects.

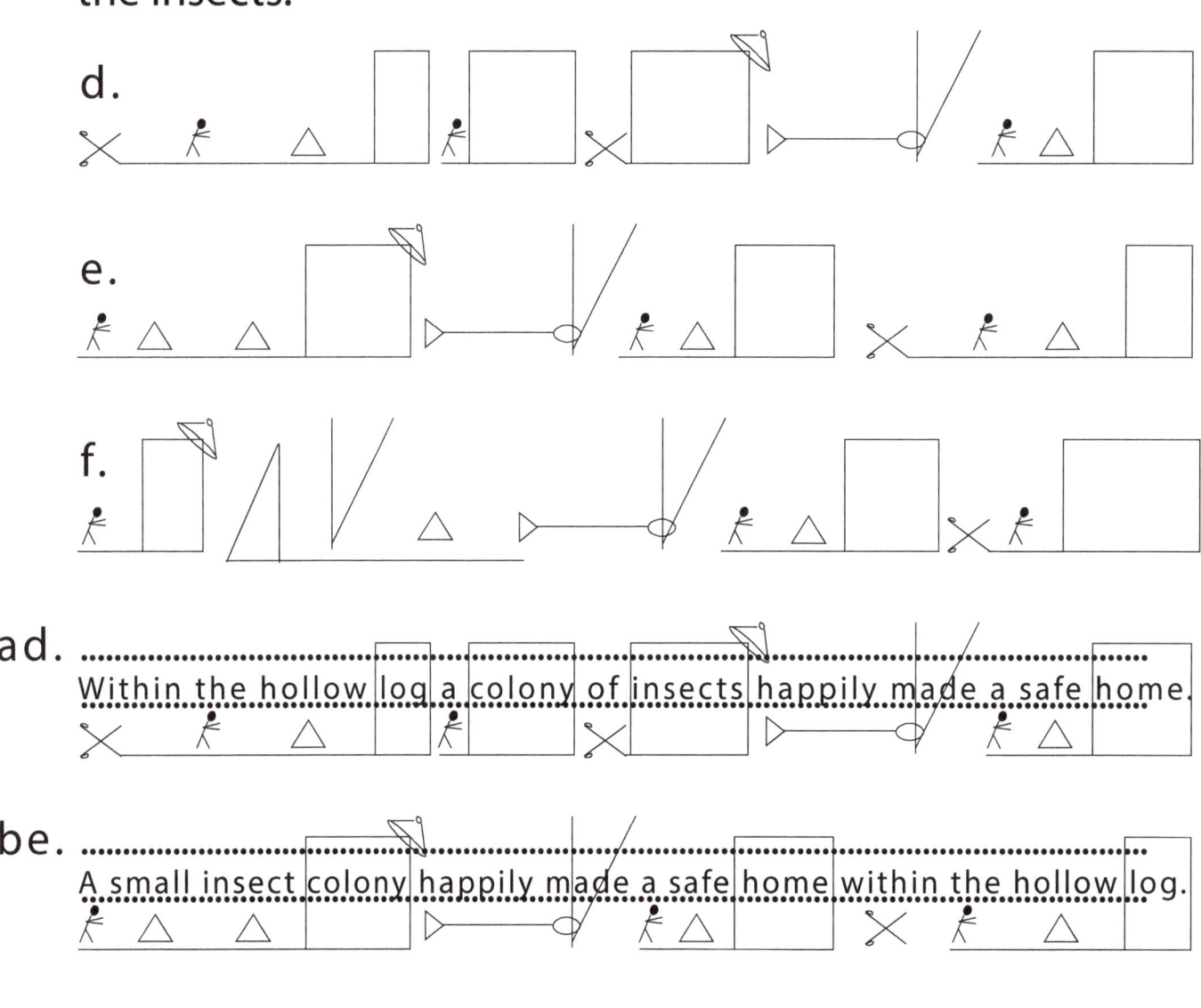

Additional Exercise (7) Answers

Match the sentences with the images. Check by adding the text

a. The famous actor had a soft pleasant face yet her voice was always harsh.

b. The actor who was famous always had a harsh voice but a pleasant face.

c. With a pleasant face the actor was famous and also known for her harshness.

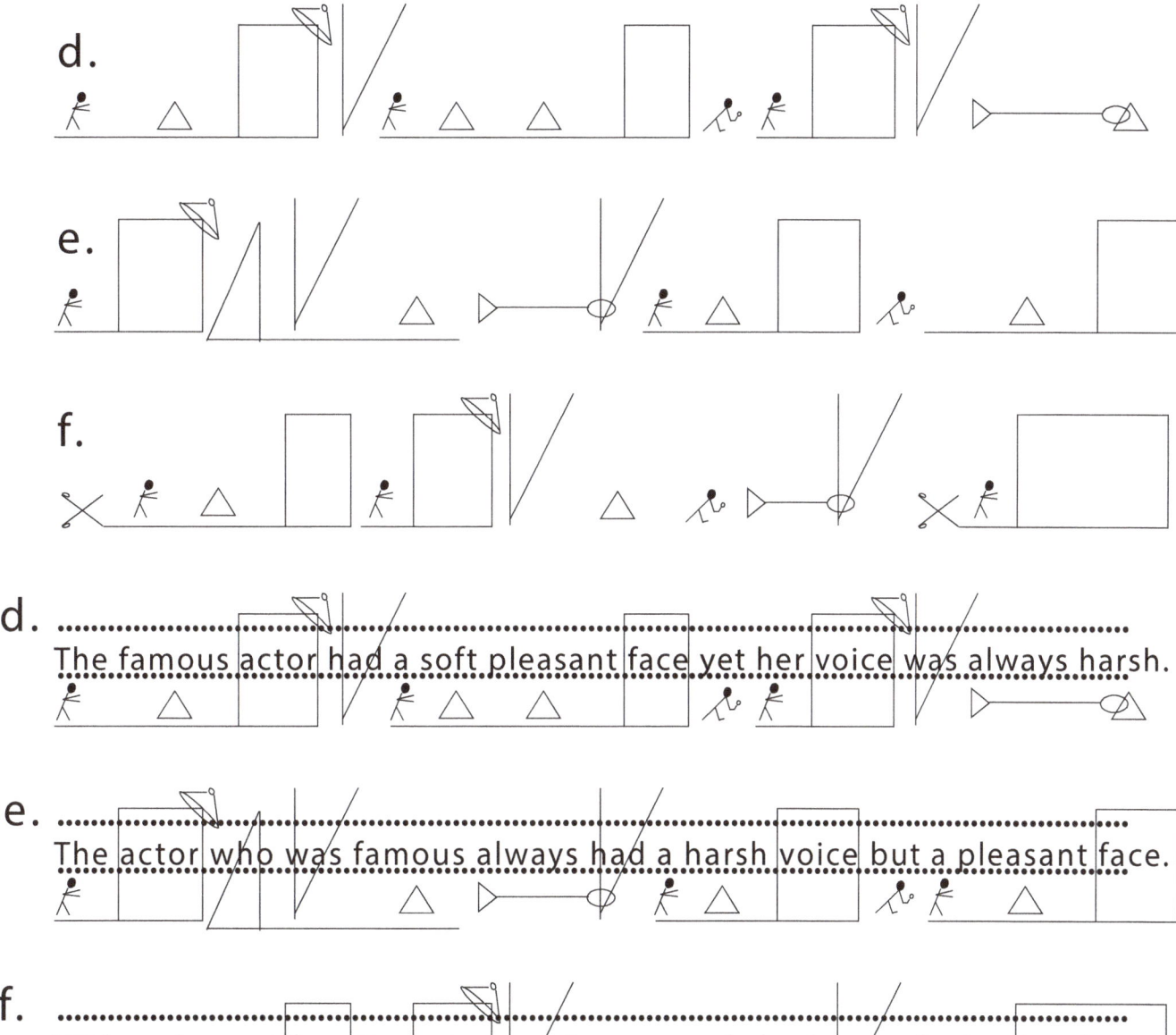

Additional Exercise (8)

SEEK & DRAW: Find the structure, draw the picture.

1. In her room, beneath the tangle of the bedclothes,

2. Tamara immediately thought Saturday.

3. The sun was brighter, the birds were chirpier and I am happier

4. mused Tamara. In the laundry Dad neatly sorted the washing:

5. bundles of colour on the green benches, piles of t-shirts

6. and mountains of patterned sheets on the tiled floor.

7. Tamara impulsively jumped into the sheets which were smelly,

8. pulled a face of disgust and laughed out loud. The mower roared

9. into life from the backyard and the cat, showing his cowardliness

10. shamelessly flew through the open doors. Nearly everyone was

11. in the overcrowded laundry. Mum remained in the garden

12. with her noisy mower and cruised happily over the grass.

Additional Exercise (8) Cont.

Seek List:

Line 1. three prepositional phrases

Line 2. one verb handled by an adverb

Line 3. three parts of the verb "to be"

Line 4. one prepositional phrase, one verb handled by an adverb

Line 5. three prepositional phrases

Line 6. two prepositonal phrases

Line 7. verb handled by the adverb, one prepositional phrase, relative pronoun clause (it will have a verb in it)

Line 8. one prepostional phrase, one verb handled by an adverb

Line 9. four nouns

Line 10. verb handled by the adverb, one prepositional phrase

Line 11. one prepositional phrase

Line 12. two prepositional phrases, one verb handled by the adverb,

Additional Exercise (8) Answers

SEEK & DRAW: Find the structure, draw the picture.

1. In her room, beneath the tangle of the bedclothes,

2. Tamara immediately thought Saturday.

3. The sun was brighter, the birds were chirpier and I am happier

4. mused Tamara. In the laundry Dad neatly sorted the washing:

5. bundles of colour on the green benches, piles of t-shirts

6. and mountains of patterned sheets on the tiled floor.

7. Tamara impulsively jumped into the sheets which were smelly,

8. pulled a face of disgust and laughed out loud. The mower roared

9. into life from the backyard and the cat, showing his cowardliness

10. shamelessly flew through the open doors. Nearly everyone was

11. in the overcrowded laundry. Mum remained in the garden

12. with her noisy mower and cruised happily over the grass.

Additional Exercise (8) Cont.

Seek List:

Line 1. three prepositional phrases

Line 2. one verb handled by an adverb

Line 3. three parts of the verb "to be"

Line 4. one prepositional phrase, one verb handled by an adverb

Line 5. three prepositional phrases

Line 6. two prepositonal phrases

Line 7. verb handled by the adverb, one prepositional phrase, relative pronoun clause (it will have a verb in it)

Line 8. one prepostional phrase, one verb handled by an adverb

Line 9. four nouns

Line 10. verb handled by the adverb, one prepositional phrase

Line 11. one prepositional phrase

Line 12. two prepositional phrases, one verb handled by the adverb,

Additional Exercise (9)

PICTURE FIND: Use your creativity and fill in the blanks. Use the images to create the complete sentence.

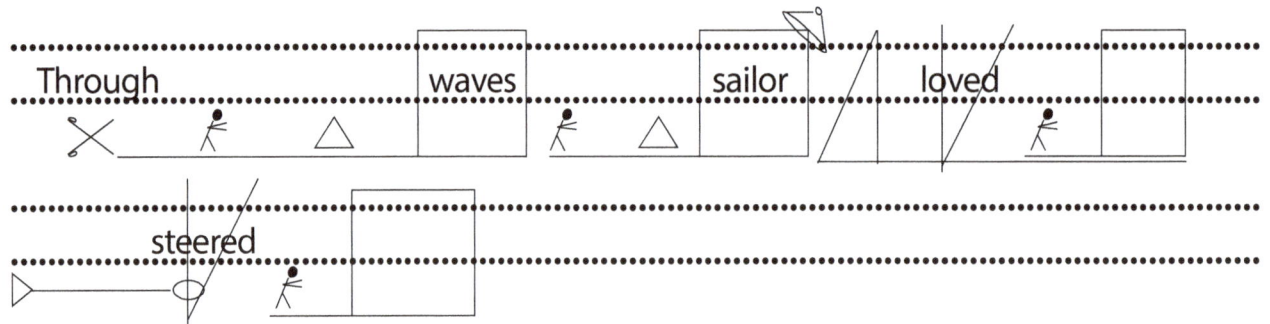

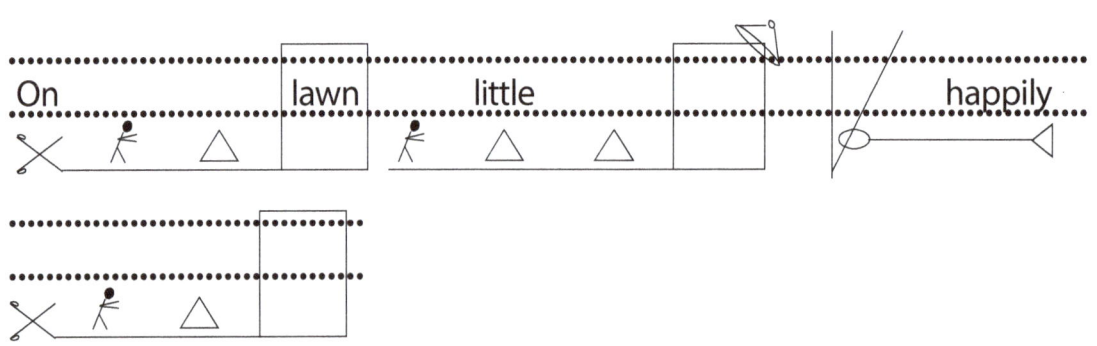

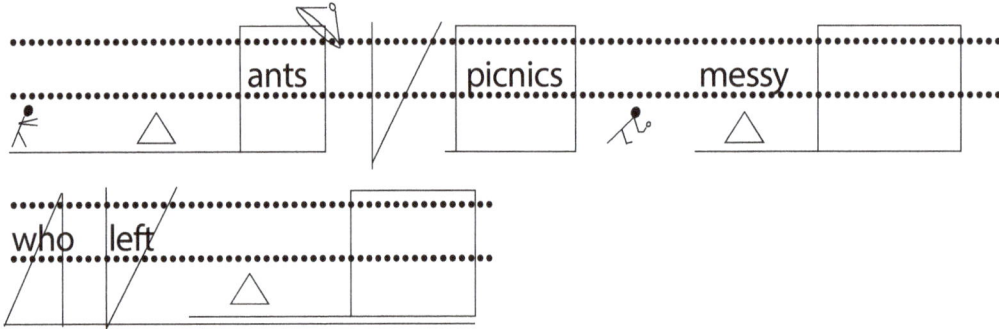

Additional Exercise (10)

PICTURE FIND: Use your creativity and fill in the blanks. Use the images to create the complete sentence.

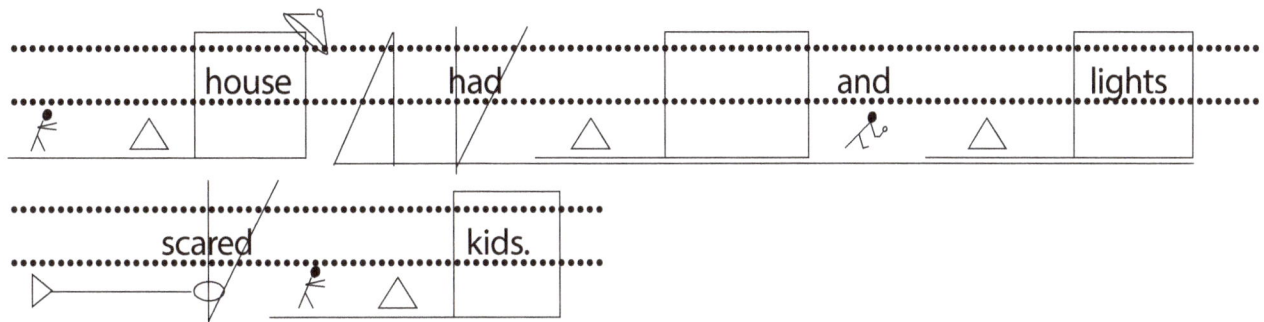

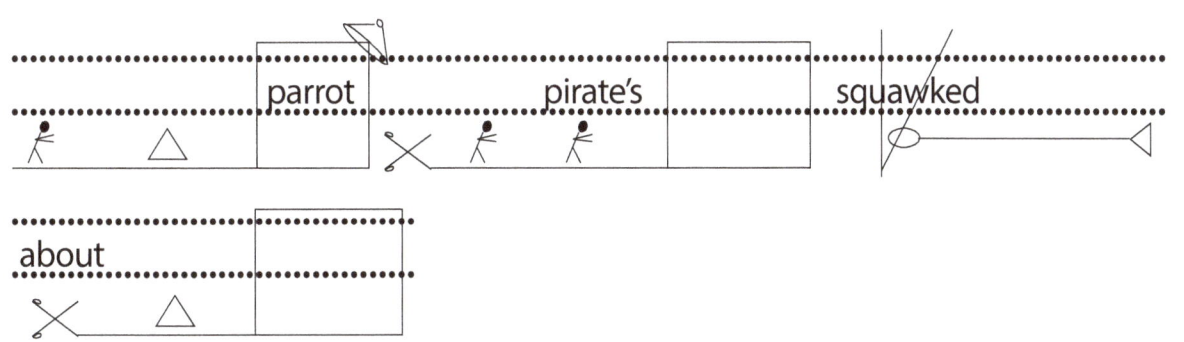

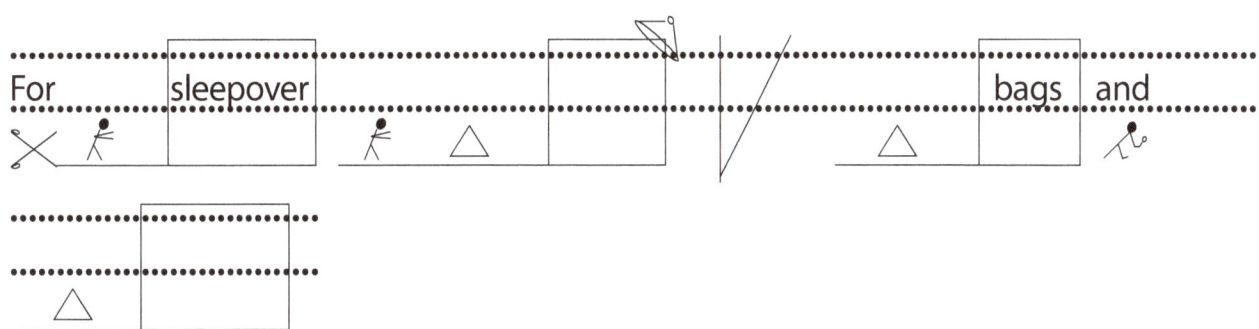

Additional Exercise (9) Answers

PICTURE FIND: Use your creativity and fill in the blanks. Use the images to create the complete sentence. Below are possible answers to the exercise.

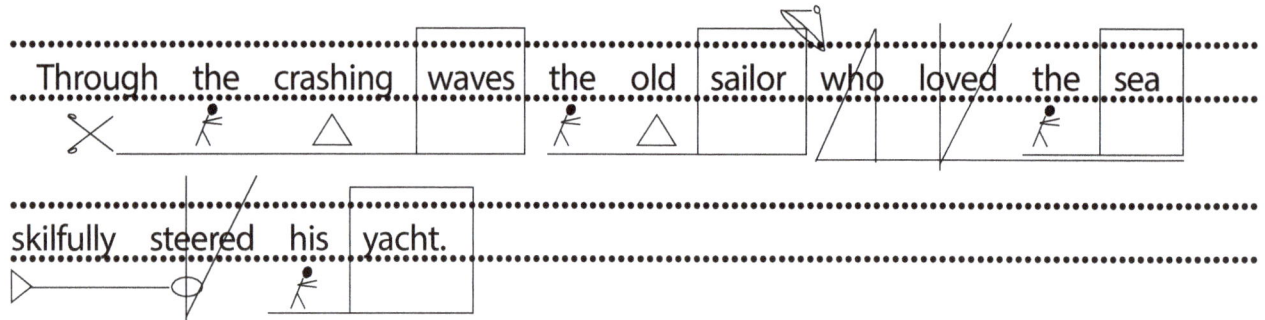

Through the crashing waves the old sailor who loved the sea skilfully steered his yacht.

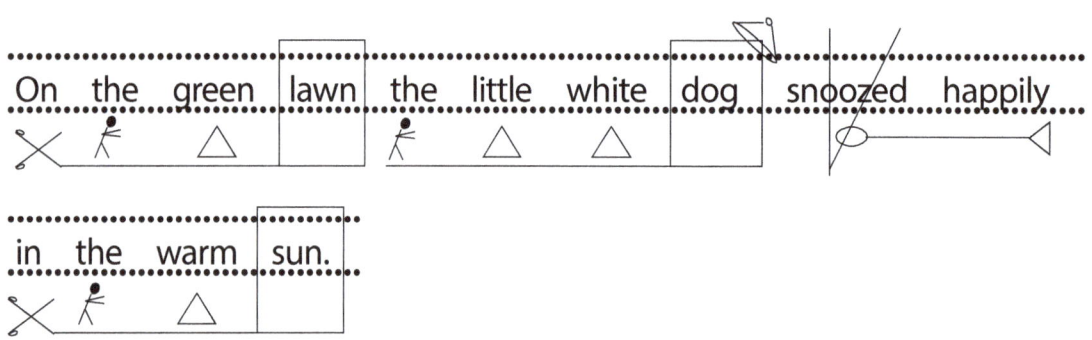

On the green lawn the little white dog snoozed happily in the warm sun.

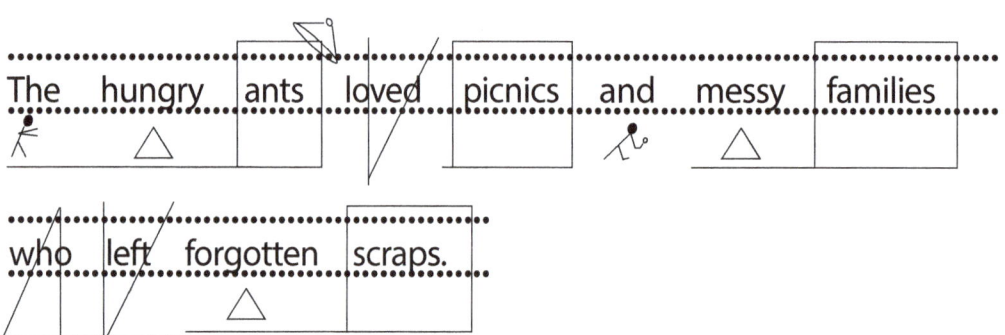

The hungry ants loved picnics and messy families who left forgotten scraps.

Additional Exercise (10) Answers

PICTURE FIND: Use your creativity and fill in the blanks. Use the images to create the complete sentence. Below are possible answers to the exercise.

The old house which had broken windows and flickering lights always scared the little kids.

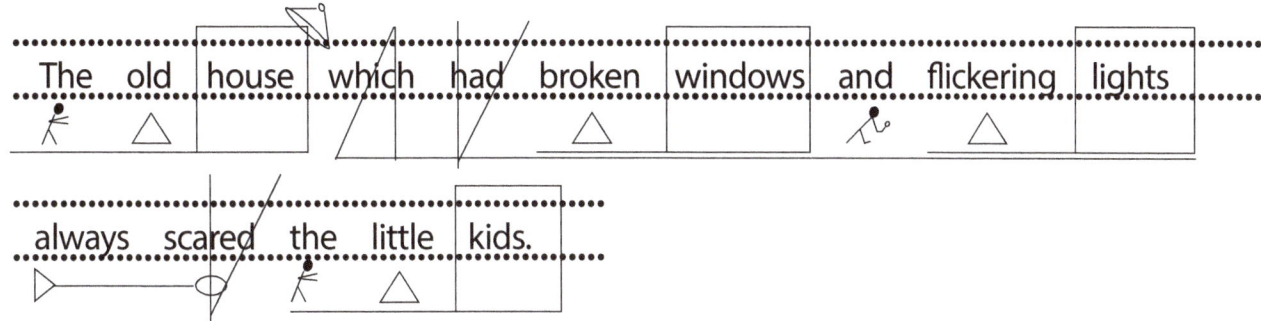

The colourful parrot on the pirate's shoulder squawked endlessly about buried treasure.

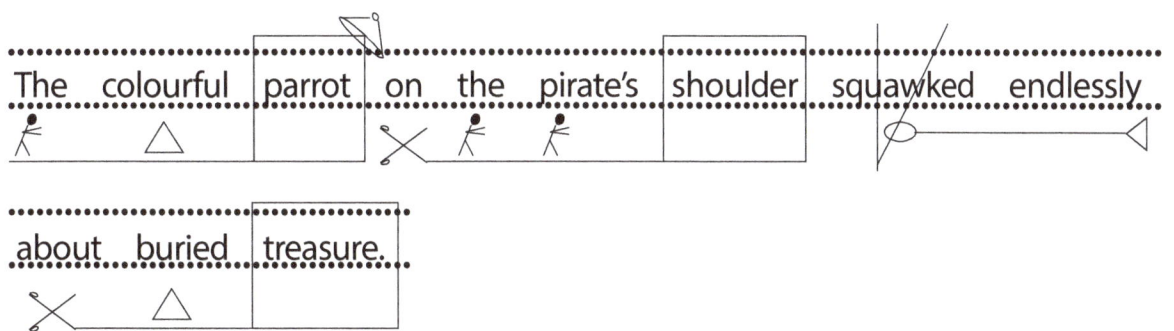

For the sleepover the excited guests brought sleeping bags and sugary snacks.

Additional Exercise (11)

SEEK & DRAW: Find the structure, draw the picture.

1. A special lunch for a special day: a special day in the holidays.

2. By their comfy home across the the small lane was a park,

3. not very big but a perfect place for Sam, who was nearly nine,

4. to be an independent girl. From the house's big windows standing

5. on kitchen steps everybody could see the adventurous Sam.

6. She opened her lunchbox which was extremely full, taking out

7. a freshly cooked sausage. A freshly cooked sausage thought Jesse,

8. the dog, Sam's constant companion. His tail was a shaking blur,

9. he snorted relentlessly. At this precise moment, Jesse leapt for the

10. sausage and he happily gulped that part of Sam's special lunch.

11. Mum laughed kindly from the kitchen window. She could

12. already see Jesse eagerly expecting Sam's ham sandwich.

Additional Exercise (11) Cont.

Seek List:

Line 1. three noun phrases using the same adjective, and a prepositional phrase at the end of the line

Line 2. two prepositional phrases

Line 3. a conjunction, one prepositional phrase, a relative pronoun clause, the verb immediately after the relative pronoun.

Line 4. one prepositional phrase

Line 5. one prepositional phrase

Line 6. a relative pronoun clause, the verb immediately after the relative pronoun, an adjective handled by an adverb

Line 7. a noun phrase with an adjective handled by an adverb, used twice

Line 8. a noun that has become a determiner

Line 9. verb handled by an adverb, one prepositional phrase

Line 10. a conjunction, a verb handled by an adverb, one prepositional phrase

Line 11. verb handled by an adverb, one prepositional phrase

Line 12. a noun that has become a determiner

Additional Exercise (11) Answers

SEEK & DRAW: Find the structure, draw the picture.

1. A special lunch for a special day; a special day in the holidays.

2. By their comfy home across the small lane was a park,

3. not very big but a perfect place for Sam, who was nearly nine,

4. to be an independent girl. From the house's big windows standing

5. on kitchen steps everybody could see the adventurous Sam.

6. She opened her lunchbox which was extremely full, taking out

7. a freshly cooked sausage. A freshly cooked sausage thought Jesse,

8. the dog, Sam's constant companion. His tail was a shaking blur,

9. he snorted relentlessly. At this precise moment, Jesse leapt for the

10. sausage and he happily gulped that part of Sam's special lunch.

11. Mum laughed kindly from the kitchen window. She could

12. already see Jesse eagerly expecting Sam's ham sandwich.

Additional Exercise (11) Cont.

Seek List:

Line 1. three noun phrases using the same adjective, and a prepositional phrase at the end of the line

Line 2. two prepositional phrases

Line 3. a conjunction, one prepositional phrase, a relative pronoun clause, the verb immediately after the relative pronoun.

Line 4. one prepositional phrase

Line 5. one prepositional phrase

Line 6. a relative pronoun clause, the verb immediately after the relative pronoun, an adjective handled by an adverb

Line 7. a noun phrase with an adjective handled by an adverb, used twice

Line 8. a noun that has become a determiner

Line 9. verb handled by an adverb, one prepositional phrase

Line 10. a conjunction, a verb handled by an adverb, one prepositional phrase

Line 11. verb handled by an adverb, one prepositional phrase

Line 12. a noun that has become a determiner

Additional Exercise (12)

Match the sentences with the images. Check by adding the text

a. Charlie the cat anxiously scouted the room in an exploration for his lost toys.

b. Charlie the anxious cat scouted the room and looked eagerly for his lost toys.

c. In a hopeful search, Charlie scouted the room for his treasures which were lost.

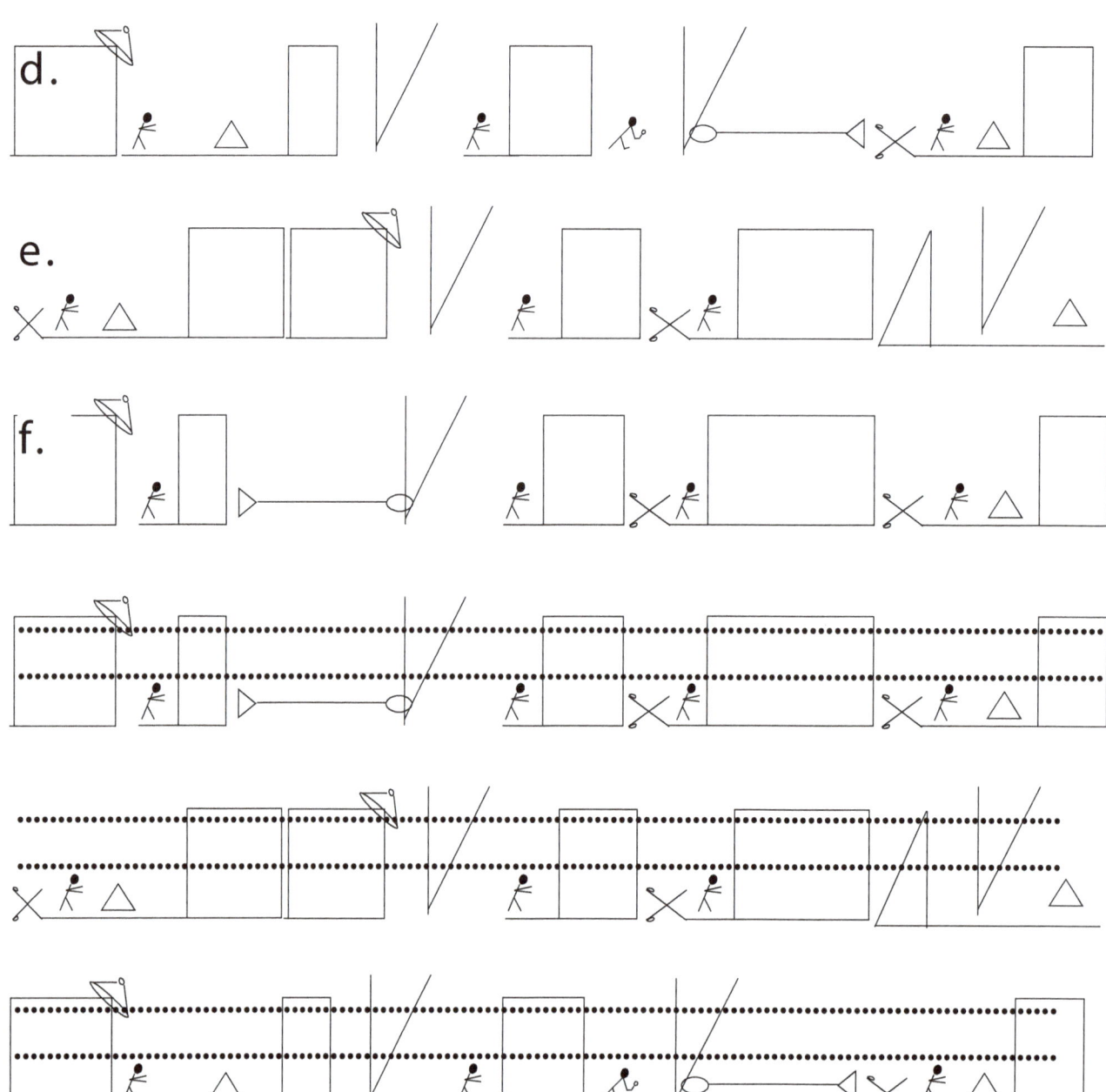

Additional Exercise (13)

Match the words with the images to create structured sentences. All of the verbs come from "to be" and "to have".

quietly the town the stranger streets through the walked On moonlit

unstoppable Campbell From secret trackers who on mountain watched the the were cave the

wonderfully which leaves The the old lemon were covered green tree of the birdbath

Additional Exercise (12) Answers

Match the sentences with the images. Check by adding the text

a. Charlie the cat anxiously scouted the room in an exploration for his lost toys.

b. Charlie the anxious cat scouted the room and looked eagerly for his lost toys.

c. In a hopeful search, Charlie scouted the room for his treasures which were lost.

d.

e.

f.

af. Charlie the cat anxiously scouted the room in an exploration for his lost toys.

bd. Charlie the anxious cat scouted the room and looked eagerly for his lost toys.

ce. In a hopeful search Charlie scouted the room for his treasures which were lost.

Additional Exercise (13) Answers

Match the words with the images to create structured sentences. All of the verbs come from "to be" and "to have".

quietly the town the stranger streets through the walked On moonlit

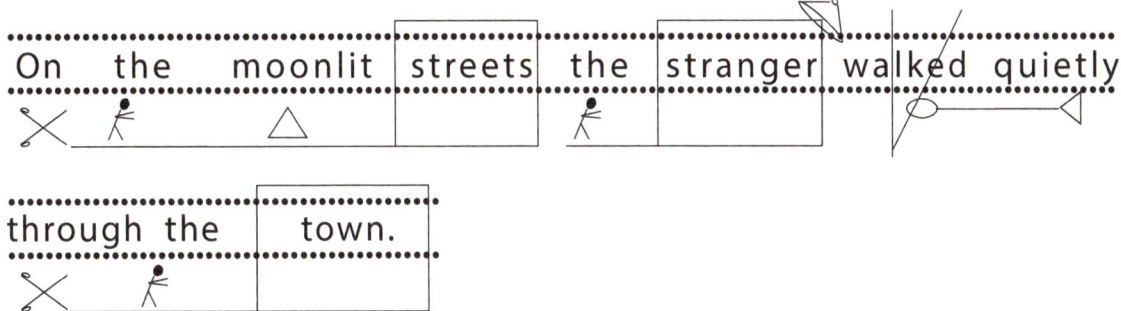

unstoppable Campbell From secret trackers who on mountain watched the the were cave the

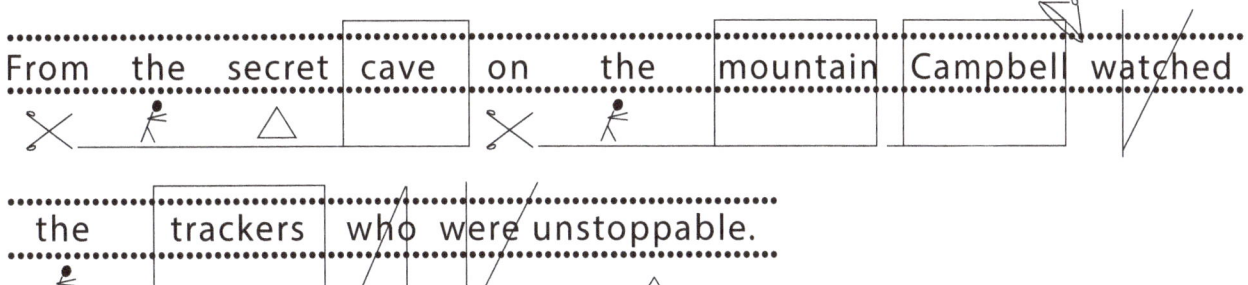

wonderfully which leaves The the old lemon were covered green tree of the birdbath

Additional Exercise (14)

SEEK & DRAW: Find the structure, draw the picture.

1. The band in frighteningly dark black denim burst onto the stage

2. which displayed a wall of heavy black amplifiers.

3. In the centre of the stage the drumkit stood on a high platform.

4. The string players carried exotic guitars and the drummer, his sticks.

5. Spotlights washed over the audience who screamed their delight

6. at the first glimpse of Shift. The concert hall was the best place

7. and Shift was the best Swedish band. John played electric guitar,

8. Eddie on bass and above their heads Tom played his drums.

9. Shift's distinctive music, of simple melodies and sonic destruction

10. always gratified their teenage fans. Security was tight. The crowd

11. pushed closer to the stage. Eddie started with a slow song

12. about a lonely bird. This brought some calm to the audience.

Additional Exercise (14) Cont.

Seek List:

Line 1. two prepositional phrases (the first phrase has an adjective handled by an adverb)

Line 2. a relative pronoun clause, the verb immediately after the relative pronoun, including the prepositional phrase

Line 3. Three prepositional phrases

Line 4. two adjectives riding on the shadows of nouns

Line 5. a relative pronoun clause, the verb immediately after the relative pronoun

Line 6. a verb from "to be"

Line 7. a noun made into an adjective

Line 8. a conjunction followed by a prepositional phrase

Line 9. a noun made into a determiner, three adjectives riding on the shadows of nouns

Line 10. a verb from "to be"

Line 11. one prepositional phrase

Line 12. two prepositional phrases

Additional Exercise (14) Answers

SEEK & DRAW: Find the structure, draw the picture.

1. The band in frighteningly dark black denim burst onto the stage
2. which displayed a wall of heavy black amplifiers.
3. In the centre of the stage the drumkit stood on a high platform.
4. The string players carried exotic guitars and the drummer, his sticks.
5. Spotlights washed over the audience who screamed their delight
6. at the first glimpse of Shift. The concert hall was the best place
7. and Shift was the best English band. John played electric guitar,
8. Eddie on bass and above their heads Tom played his drums.
9. Shift's distinctive music, of simple melodies and sonic destruction
10. always gratified their teenage fans. Security was tight. The crowd
11. pushed closer to the stage. Eddie started with a slow song
12. about a lonely bird. This brought some calm to the audience.

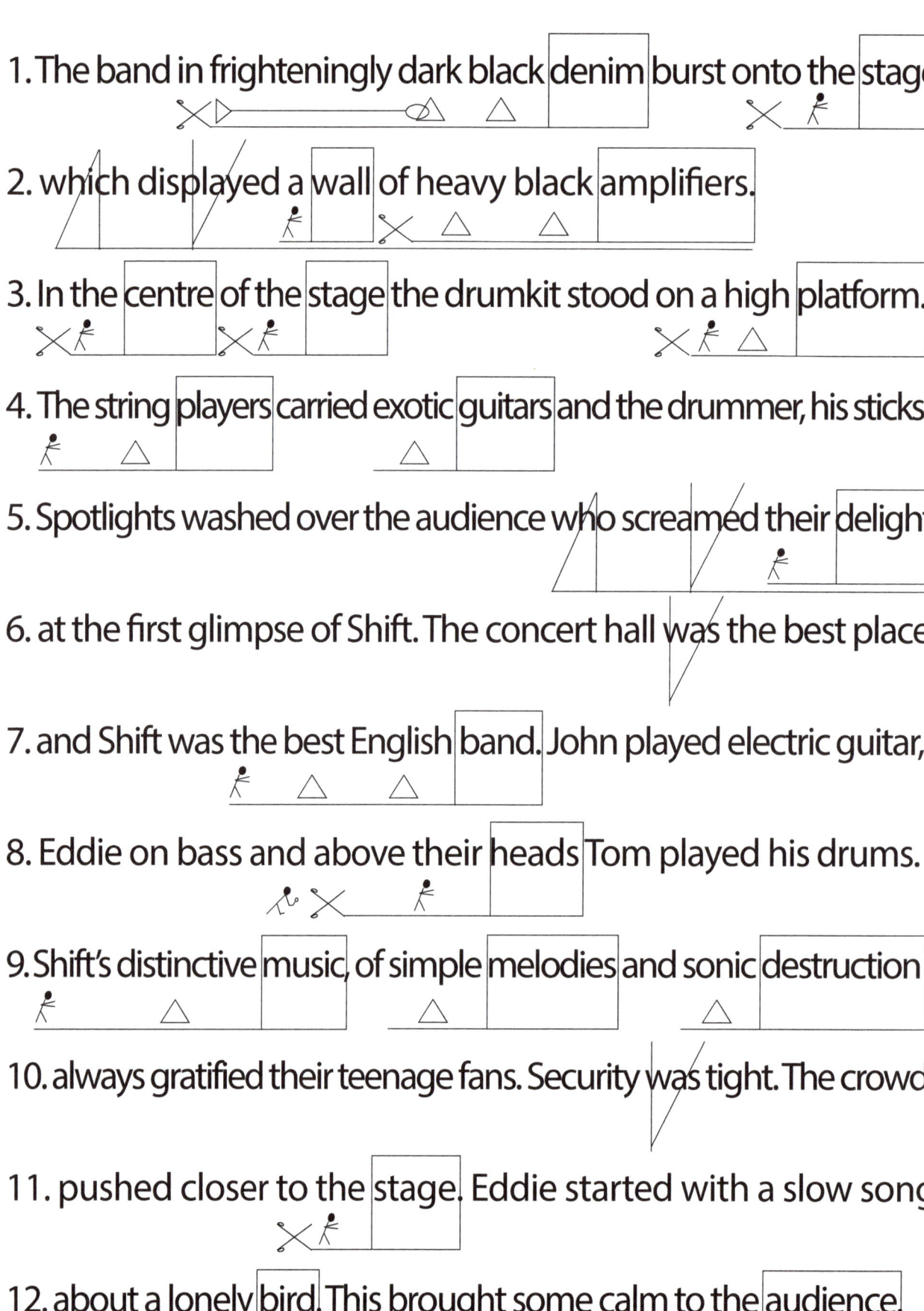

Additional Exercise (14) Cont.

Seek List:

Line 1. two prepositional phrases (the first phrase has an adjective handled by an adverb)

Line 2. a relative pronoun clause, the verb immediately after the relative pronoun, including the prepositional phrase

Line 3. Three prepositional phrases

Line 4. two adjectives riding on the shadows of nouns

Line 5. a relative pronoun clause, the verb immediately after the relative pronoun

Line 6. a verb from "to be"

Line 7. a noun made into an adjective

Line 8. a conjunction followed by a prepositional phrase

Line 9. a noun made into a determiner, three adjectives riding on the shadows of nouns

Line 10. a verb from "to be"

Line 11. one prepositional phrase

Line 12. two prepositional phrases

Additional Exercise (15)

PICTURE FIND: Use your creativity and fill in the blanks. Use the images to create the complete sentence.

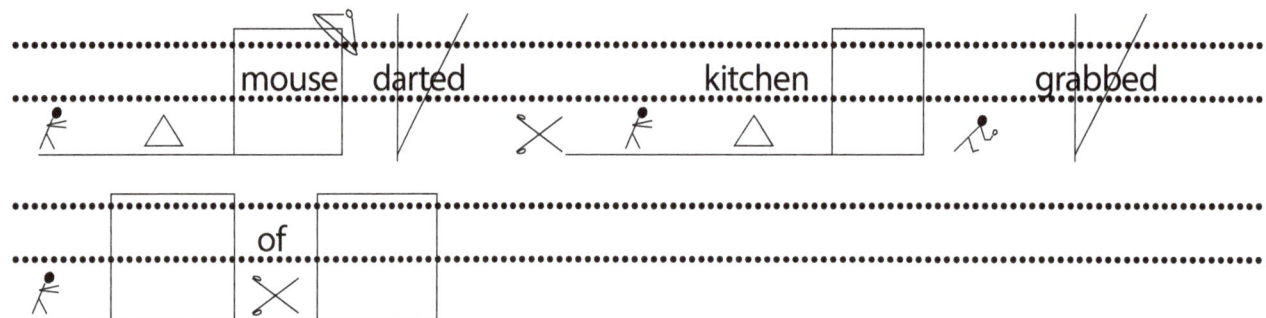

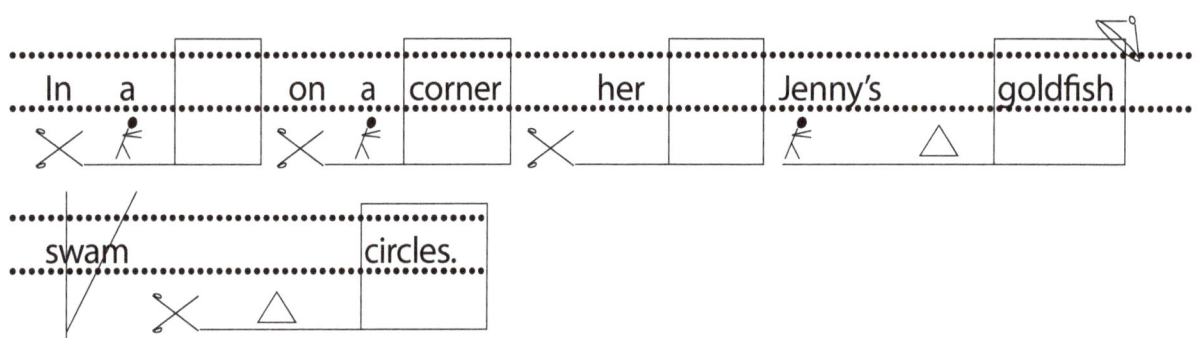

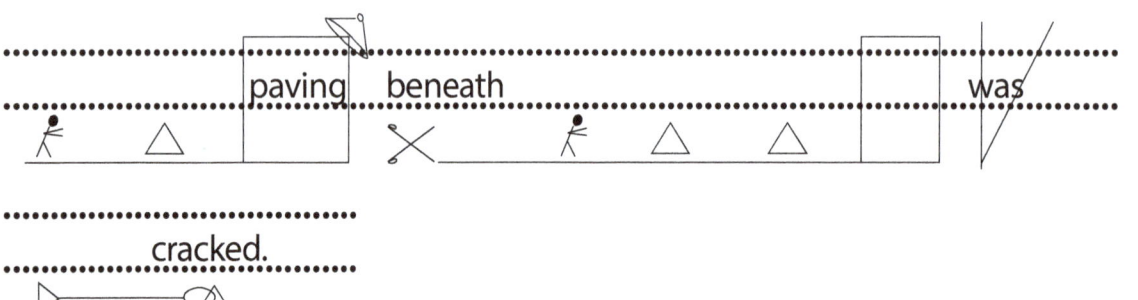

Additional Exercise (16)

PICTURE FIND: Use your creativity and fill in the blanks. Use the images to create the complete sentence.

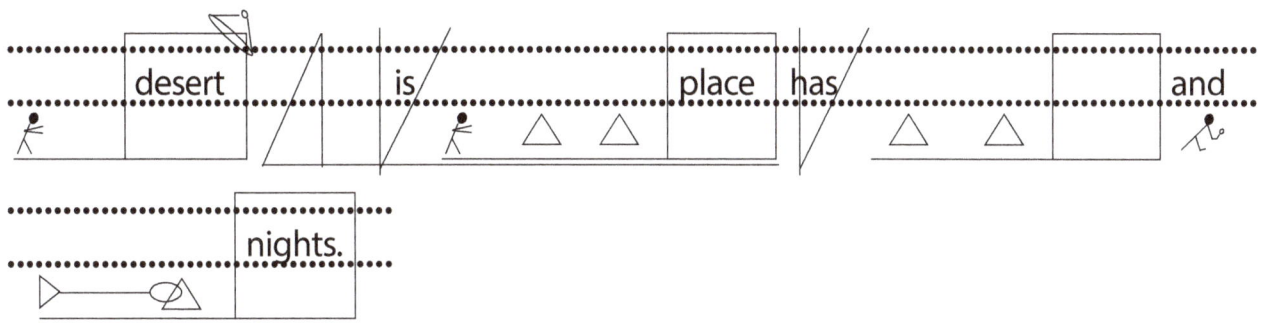

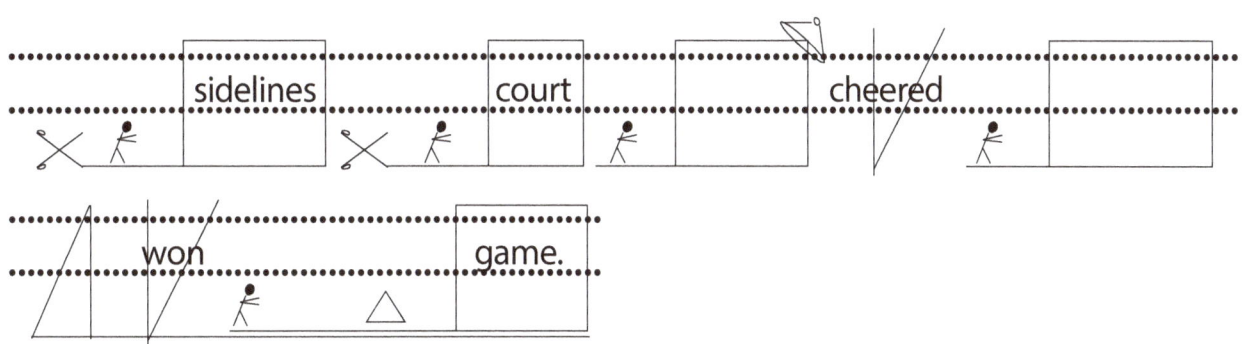

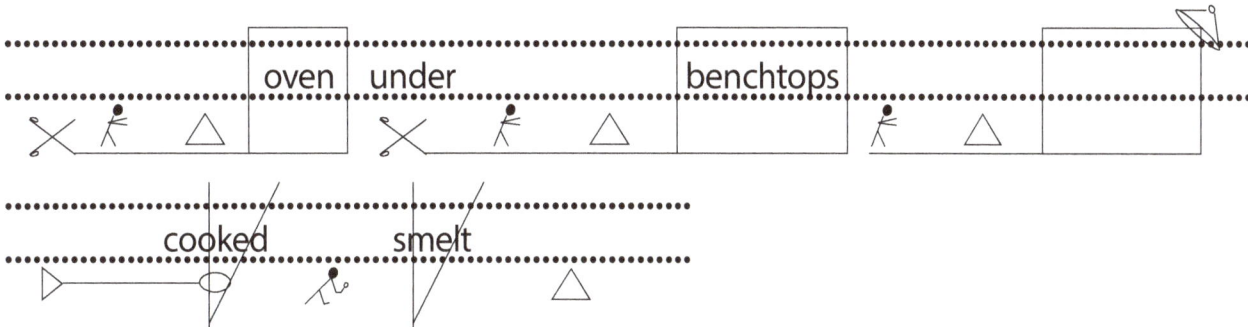

■ Additional Exercise (15) Answers

PICTURE FIND: Use your creativity and fill in the blanks. Use the images to create the complete sentence. Below are possible answers to the exercise.

The brave mouse darted across the kitchen floor and grabbed the crumb of cheese.

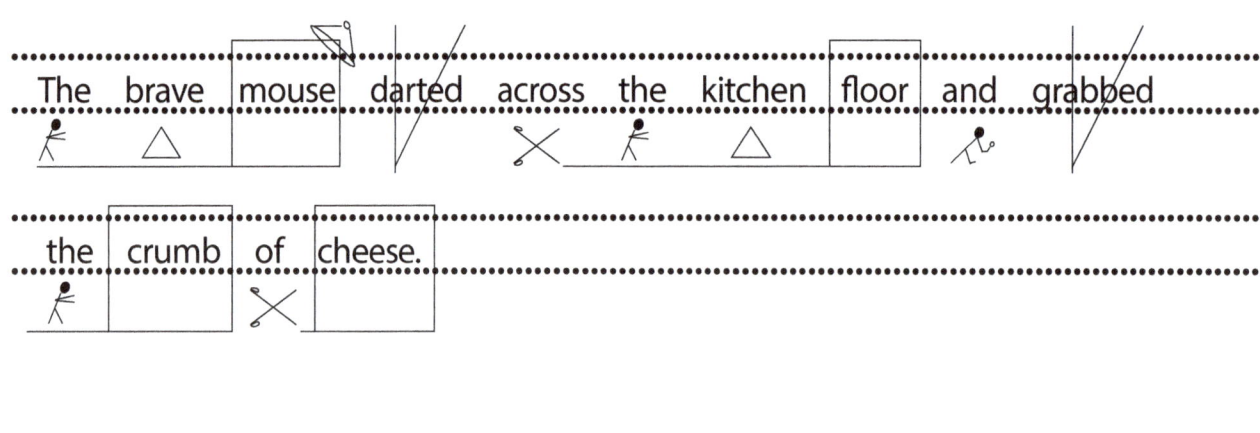

In a bowl on a corner of her desk Jenny's pet goldfish swam in endless circles.

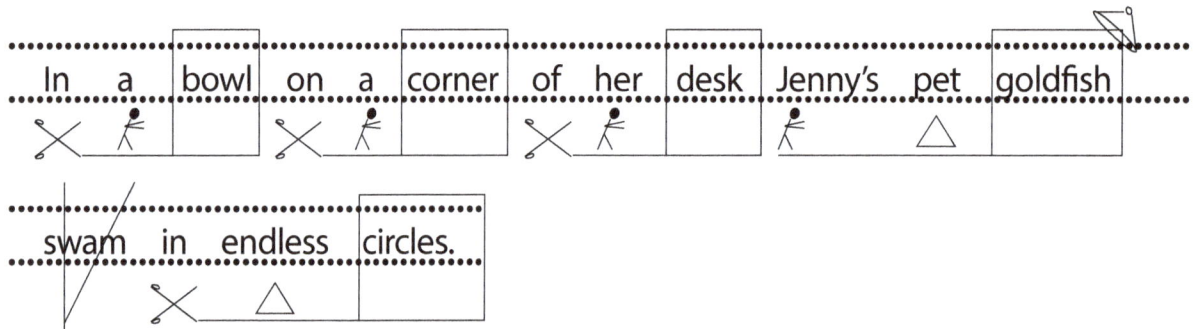

The stone paving beneath the large shady tree was badly cracked.

PAGE 98

Additional Exercise (16) Answers

PICTURE FIND: Use your creativity and fill in the blanks. Use the images to create the complete sentence. Below are possible answers to the exercise.

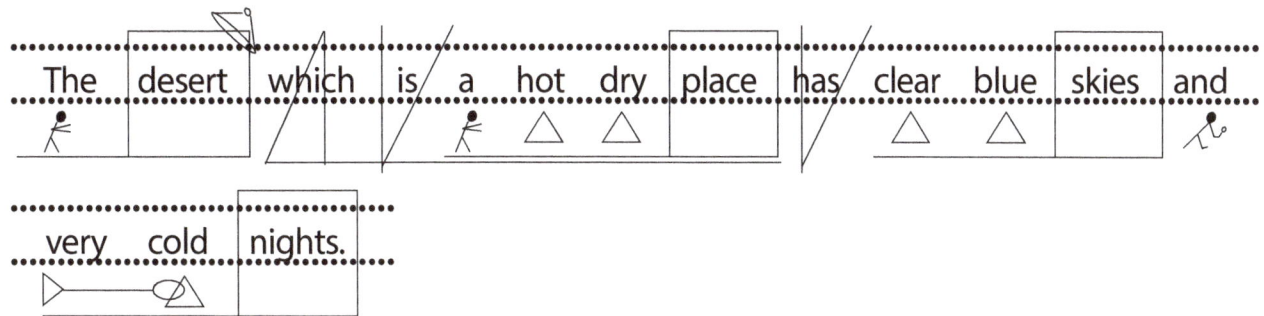

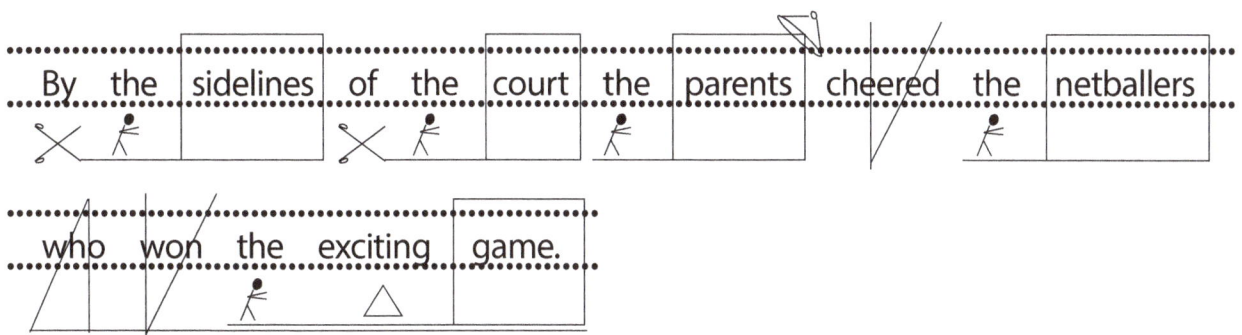

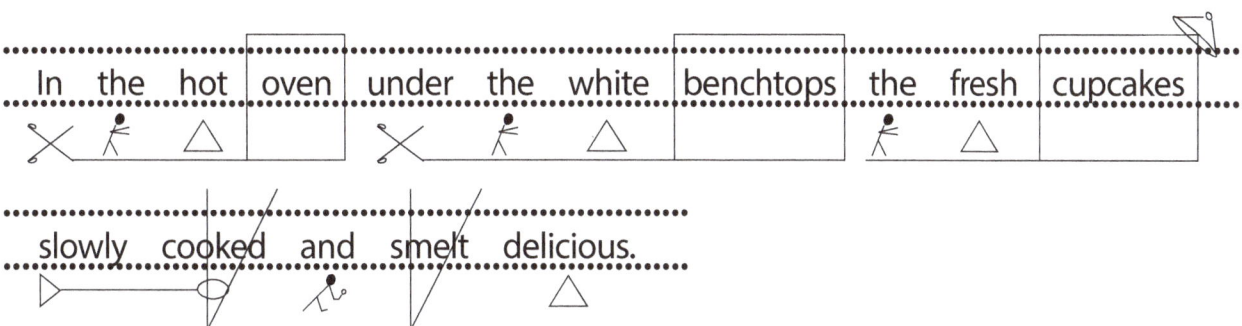

GRAMMAR Made Easy

Glossary

Here you will find a list of all the pictures we have covered so far.

"Pictorial Grammar Theory is a useful tool for learning English grammar"

PAGE
101

Glossary of Pictures

Book 1 - Beginner

Picture Number	Picture	Description
1	▢	Noun
2	◁	Spotlight
3	▢ (with shadow)	The Shadow On The Noun
4	(stick figure)	The Determiner
5	△	The Adjective
6	✕	The Preposition
7	V	The Verb
8a	▷—△	The Adverb with Adjectives
8b	▷—⌀	The Adverb with Verbs
9	(stick figure)	The Conjunction
10	◿	The Relative Pronoun & It's Clause

The Pictorial Grammar Theory Series

Book 1: Beginner

Book 2: Intermediate

Book 3: Professional

Book 4: Expert

Book 5: Master

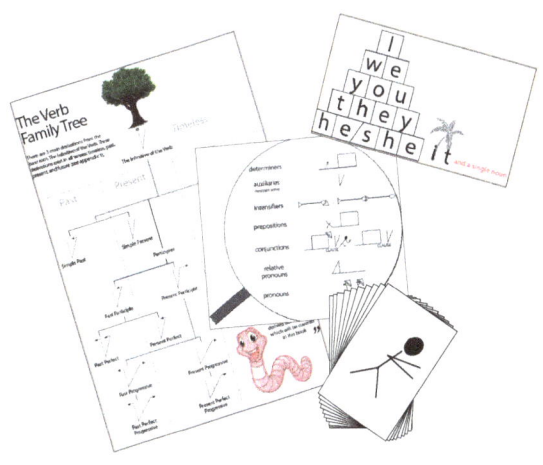

And additional resources at
www.profstripes.com

www.ingramcontent.com/pod-product-compliance
Lightning Source LLC
Chambersburg PA
CBHW061537010526
44107CB00067B/2899